I0801265

Praise for Nicole Gabriel and *Stepping Into Your Becoming*:

"Every now and again a book enters your consciousness and its wisdom forever changes your life. This is one of those books! Full of practical wisdom, *Stepping into Your Becoming* will unleash a newfound confidence in you that will allow you to stand in your authentic power and overcome all life's adversities. Apply this book's teachings to your soul and you will become unstoppable!"

— Patrick Snow, International Best-Selling Author of *Creating Your Own Destiny*, *The Affluent Entrepreneur*, and *Boy Entrepreneur*

"Love, loss, and even anger can motivate you to make a change, and this book will show you not only how, but guide you on what to do next."

— Jeff Bow, Life Coach and
Author of *Stop Thinking, Start Believing*

"In *Stepping into Your Becoming*, Nicole Gabriel takes readers on an internal journey to find and own their authentic selves. Her method of seeing the world around her as a mirror of herself full of lessons to learn from will change how many people see the world, and that new perspective will lead to powerful change not only for themselves but for all with whom they interact."

— Tyler R. Tichelaar, Ph.D., and Award-Winning
Author of The Children of Arthur series

"Keep a copy of *Stepping Into Your Becoming* nearby. You will want to refer to it often! Dive into Nicole's book and let your healing transformation begin."

— Suzan H. Proia, EPC, C.Ht., Author of
Finding Your Answers Within

"Take this journey with Nicole and step deeper into the consciousness of your self—open up to greater personal transformation and the possibilities that your life can offer!"

— Lyla Berg, Ph.D., Keynote Speaker, Resiliency Consultant, and
Author of *Leaving the Gilded Cage*

"If you've ever been through a change in your life, whether it be spiritual or not, you're going to want to get this book!"

— Luis De La Fuente, Author of
Life Lessons from the Lantern

"This book compiles the humanology and healing practices of many backgrounds, technologies, spiritual practices, and cultures to showcase many ways to transform oneself into a strong leader of self to guide others."

— Jonathon Wong, MBA, M.ED, MPA,
Author of *Succeeding in College and Life*

"Let Nicole help you get further down the roads of life as she teaches that divine self-love is the ultimate truth."

— Jim Jacobs, Author of
Driving Lessons for Life

"Through her experiences, Nicole pinpointed the exact moment to produce the perfect book for our times, yet it is timeless. Humanity needs this book now, and it has arrived just in time!"

— Nora Young, Author of
Healing Effortlessly

"*Stepping Into Your Becoming* teaches how to be thankful, to experience living in the moment, and to be grateful for all life situations."

— Laurel Winston, Author of
Carrots Grow from Carrot Seeds

"I've done a lot of healing in my life, but this book taught me that I really wasn't ever wounded to begin with once I learned how to shift my mind."

— Jeremy Wallace, Author of
Taking the Scenic Route to Manhood

"I've been on a spiritual transformational path for years, but this book took everything I've learned and transformed it into a more positive place."

— Susan Ortolano, Author of
Re-Marrying Right

"A dazzling journey with Nicole. Opening the mind and soul on the simplicity of walking a spiritual path mindfully and with ease."

— Ila Barlean, Author of *Her Being*

"This book teaches one to open up to deep levels of love and happiness and guides one to empower a strong belief in self."

— Brett Dupree, Author of
Joyous Expansion

"*Stepping Into Your Becoming* teaches that when you learn to open up to the voice within and live according to your own internal guidance, everything that is divinely guided will show up for you as it's intended."

— Natalie Kawai, Author of
Conversations With Mother Goddess

"*Stepping Into Your Becoming* combines so many cultural and spiritual backgrounds together into one book that guides one into a place of transformation."

— Sally Holmes Reed, Co-Author of
The Change Book 1, Chapter 15, Channel Your Success

"Embracing and expanding upon the Law of Attraction, this book will teach you how to live in a way that surrounds you with positive, supportive people, and it will help you realize the life you've always dreamed of, but never thought possible."

— Matthew D. Dubin, Seattle Attorney and
Author of *Maximizing Your Injury Claim*

"Nicole has a strong connection to the spirit world—making her information authentic, insightful, and thought-provoking. The content she provides here will move you through life challenges into self-discovery and assist you in finding personal freedom."

— David Armstrong, Author of
Messages from the Spirit World

"When you read Nicole's book, you'll discover how to shift your thinking. Doing so then shifts your vibration, which leads to attracting beautiful things into your life. And who doesn't want beautiful things? If you do, this is a must read!"

— Debra Jason, Best-Selling Author of
Millionaire Marketing on a Shoestring Budget™

"Nicole so wonderfully leads you through the inner journey of transformation and authenticity. Stepping into becoming in my life has connected me to walking in trust and surrender to all the wonder of life and all the magic that is within us and around us."

— Lisa Ulshafer, Author of *Journey with an Angel*

"As a travel writer, I'm always on a journey, but thanks to Nicole, I learned some new trips. Find this fabulous book, and step into YOUR becoming."

— Karen Jeffery, Author of *My Little French Diary,*
Cuba Notes, Hot Tickets!! - A Week on Maui,
Neosomaniac, Coconut Cuisine

"If you have been searching with little or no success for happiness, maybe it is time to look inside. Nicole does an amazing job with, "Stepping Into Your Becoming" by embarking on the journey beside you and guides you along the way. What you discover will amaze you. Pick up your copy today!"

— Autumn Shields Author of *Living Your Life Alive*

"Nicole openly takes you through a journey of love. It is with this divine awakening that leads you here to find the truth. You will learn to transform your spiritual connection to your soul by being your authentic self."

— Charmaine Lee, CHt., Author of
Becoming an Empowered Leader

"The universe is transformation;
our life is what our thoughts make it."

— Marcus Aurelius

AWAKEN — TRANSFORM — REALIZE

STEPPING INTO YOUR *Becoming*

LEADERSHIP PRINCIPLES FOR EMBRACING CHANGE AND ACHIEVING SELF MASTERY

NICOLE GABRIEL

AVIVA PUBLISHING
New York

Stepping Into Your Becoming

Leadership Principles For Embracing Change and Achieving Self Mastery

Copyright © 2015 by Nicole Gabriel

Published by:
Aviva Publishing
Lake Placid, NY
(518) 523-1320
www.AvivaPubs.com

All Rights Reserved. No part of this book may be used or reproduced in any manner whatsoever without expressed written permission of the author. Address all inquiries to:

Nicole Gabriel
Telephone (808) 280-5559
www.NicoleKristinGabriel.com
www.SteppingIntoYourBecoming.com
www.Vegan-DogTreats.com
www.AngelDogProductions.com

ISBN: 978-1-943164202
Library of Congress: 2015908419

Editor: Tyler Tichelaar
Cover Design: Angel Dog Productions
Interior Book Design: Angel Dog Productions

Every attempt has been made to source properly all quotes.
Printed in the United States of America
First Edition
2 4 6 8 10 12

To my fiancé, Patrick Snow:
Thank you for supporting me and encouraging me
to write this book. You're an awesome book coach!
(You can find him at www.ThePublishingDoctor.com
if you want help writing your book, too!)

To my parents, Chuck and Merilyn Case
I love you both!
I acknowledge our time together is growing shorter, and
I appreciate it more now than ever.

In loving memory of my canine companions
Tia, Mai Tai, Sangria, Shiitake, and Sushi.

To my "Three Musketeers" Leilani, Bella, and Blue
I know you are more than just dogs!
One day others will know animals are angels too.

To the reader, may your journey
be filled with love and light.

Acknowledgments

I would like to recognize and thank the following people for their love, support, encouragement, and/or belief in me or my message. You have touched me more than you know.

David Armstrong, Jeff Bow, The Case Family, The Craton Family, all my clients because your journey always helps focus mine, Meg Edmondson, Brodi Goshi, Lauren Long, Jo Rayl, The Snow Family, Lisa Ulshafer, Kat Weesies

To those who helped me create this book: Susan Friedmann, Todd Hobbs, Marlana Pruitt

I would like to thank the Wailuku Fire Department for their rescue efforts with Bella.

I would like to give a special thank you to my editor, Tyler Tichelaar. Without his expertise and patience, this book would not be what it is today. Trust me. He's a miracle worker!

CONTENTS

THE PLUMERIA PRAYER

The plumeria flower on the cover represents so much for me. When my Chinese Shar Pei Shiitake was sick, she wasn't able to hike up the big mountain near our home in the Iao Valley here on Maui, so instead of bringing her, I picked up a fallen plumeria flower from a nearby tree. When reaching the summit, I would blow all my prayers into the flower and leave it on a yellow fire hydrant—which seemed fitting to me.

After some time, and Shiitake's passing, I still made the hike and still picked up a flower. Each day, I would hike up the mountain with her and with all of my other loved ones who were represented in those flowers. I prayed for every person I knew, whether he or she needed it or not. I also prayed for myself. I released emotional pains and said prayers as I asked for our suffering to cease.

After some more time, I would hike up and run down as fast as I could. It was almost as if I were running away from all of my sorrows and pain. Each time, I ran down faster, and each day, after Shititake's passing, she would tell me it was time to write. She held me in spirit and guided each word that hit each page as I wrote my first book, *Finding Your Inner Truth.*

It wasn't until my heart was healed and that book was written that it became apparent to me that all those I have loved and lost were the guides to both that book and now this one. I began to become thankful, in some strange way, for their loss. Without their departure, I wouldn't have been able to write these words. I gift you with the plumeria in the hopes that it will also be a symbol of

transformation for you. So with this plumeria, make a wish, make a prayer, let go of something that no longer serves you, and say thank you to all those who guide you on your way, whether they be in spirit or not. Know that God made you perfect exactly as you are and happiness is your birthright.

Introduction

Listening to the Voice Within

Have you been on a journey to find your authentic self? Have you journeyed deeper and deeper and still come up short on who you are or who you are meant to be? Have you studied a particular spiritual technology or method only to find yourself surrounded by other people who are also trying to find themselves—others with deep wounds? Have you shifted your career, your spiritual practice, your family, yourself in such a way that nothing (even you) was recognizable? You are not alone on your journey! Many other people have gone through a shift in consciousness and character and tried to become better people but gotten lost in the effort. But this book is about so much more than being lost—its about getting found and living your purpose!

I want to help you find the true essence of your Self. I understand you believe you have suffered at various points in your life or you may be suffering in some aspect now, but I have struggled with identifying my life purpose for many years, so I understand where you are and what you are going through. I have compassion for you. I want to help guide you. You and I are much more the same than we are different.

Honestly, I have written this book, first of all, to help myself heal. But I also know that by helping myself, I am helping you and many others. We are one in the same, as I will explain as we go. When I set out to write this book, I sat down at the computer and had a conversation with God. I put my hands on the keyboard and said, "Teach me." These are the words that flowed through me as I asked God to mend my broken heart, to heal my perceived wounds from my past, and to direct me toward the next stages of my life. I was ready to heal. During my writing process, I was also guided to research some aspects of how I was guided; I got lost in what was research and what was channeled through the divine. And now I am ready to share that knowledge with you. I pray that it helps heal you as it has me.

Just a few years ago, I stepped out of divorce, the loss of many loved ones, and into a new life on the other side of the world in Maui, Hawaii. I was trying very hard to move on with my life, but each time I asked for the healing to happen, I was shown more things that needed to be healed. I don't know if our healing ever truly can be called complete, but the attitude we have about it can change. If we perceive ourselves to have wounds, and we ask for those wounds to be healed, then we will attract more of the like…meaning we will have wounds shown to us that we need to heal. If we step into this healing process as a life experience, then the concept of it being a wound changes. My first book, *Finding Your Inner Truth,* talks briefly about this process if you'd like to start there. The book you are now reading was written as a kind of sequel to it because I believe that after you have found your truth, it is easier to step into your becoming.

What do I mean by "stepping into your becoming?" Prior to approaching my divorce, I had been sitting in a meditation when I heard a voice very clearly say to me, "It's now time to step into your becoming." I slightly opened my eyes and looked around, as if asking, "Who, me?" I wasn't sure at the time what that phrase even meant. Was some bright light going to come out of the sky and give me superhuman powers? Blaze a golden road for me to step on in all my glory as I skipped off to Oz? Part of me thought this was ridiculous, but another part of me thought I must have reached a kind of plateau in my spiritual curiosities (because at that stage it would have been a stretch to call what I was doing "studies"). Either way, it seemed as if it were a kind of rite of passage. But what exactly did this voice really mean?

Oh, my goodness, was I naive about what was in store for me those next few years! I went through the most trying times of my entire life! But, thank goodness for that little voice in the back of my head that kept hearing those words because those words got me through. I knew that if I just trusted in the concept that I was simply shaking out what didn't work, I would be graced with what would. When I look back upon this time many years later now, I almost see it as if I had a kind of life seizure. It was a time that shook me to the core, but in the end, it was my faith in that little voice (and in myself) for victoriously surviving through that phase that ultimately gave me a kind of internal strength that is now mine.

I now own my strength and I survived a challenge, and no one, no one, can take that away from me. So if I were to describe today what "stepping into your becoming" really means, it means stepping into your authentic self and your authentic power. But it also means rolling with the punches, striving to be the best self you can be, and having faith you will, with the grace of God, land on your feet as a more powerful, aware, gracefully divine you. And now I can say to any challenge I'm faced with, "It's okay because I know God's got my back and I know am powerful, strong, and I can get through it!"

But I also know "your becoming" is when you consciously choose how to live your life, decide what *you* believe in, and become fully responsible for *everything* in your life. It's when you choose your path and then *"walk your talk"* and *"talk your walk."* It's when you become aware of the reflection of self in all things and respond by giving more of what you want to see back with conscious awareness. It's about taking conscious responsibility for your own actions, harnessing your power, and stepping through the challenging, but it's also at the heart of true freedom.

"With great power comes great responsibility"

— *Spider-Man* (2002 movie)

It's time to see the past as healed experiences, step beyond your fears, and step into the power of your greatness. God divinely appointed you to have the most amazing gifts, so it's time you used them to step into your becoming! What are you waiting for? It all begins with a choice.

Of course, I know that making that choice is not easy, but I hope that just as I sought and found answers through my experiences, that my sharing them with you in these pages will help you step further away from depression, confusion, and the "can'ts" and into a place of the "cans."

So you understand better where I'm coming from, let me tell you a bit more about myself. I have an MBA in Technology Management and spent the first part of my adult life working my way up the corporate ladder and into executive management in the auto industry in Detroit. I never felt at home in either Detroit or in the big, dark, gray buildings where my livelihood was earned. For many years, I slaved my way through working for someone else. But I always felt a deeper calling to find myself—the true essence of my spirit—and to learn what I really came to earth to do. I spent many years first bouncing around in my corporate jobs and then bouncing around in my personal life as I transitioned into a more spiritual person and awakened my consciousness. I also grew to know what to do and what not to do in business. Today, I own a successful graphic design company, but it wasn't easy to get here.

I traveled all over Central and South America working with Shamanic Healers in order to heal from my perceived wounds. As I journeyed deeper into myself, I discovered even more wounds until I believed I was a really broken person. Few people in my spiritual communities told me nothing was wrong with me; most offered to show me all my faults and what I needed to do to "fix" myself. After years and years of struggling with depression, I realized, in a series of moments over time, as described in this book, that I really wasn't broken; I was simply looking at things all wrong. I had conquered a lot, and I was stronger for making my way through it. I was not broken at all; in fact, I was open to the idea of having faith when everything else seemed to fail me. It wasn't one event, but a series of events over the course of my life, that led me to believe I was still here for a reason. I didn't throw in the towel because I knew I had something to learn and something to share. I survived many things in my career and personal life that I now understand as simply "gaining experience." I also came to realize: Wow, I guess I have a lot of experience. I'm a master of experience! You are, too, I bet.

In this book, you are going to walk through awakening and into transformation, realizing, and finally, being. I will share with you some of my stories of stepping into my becoming; I will teach you how change, loss, trauma, love, and anger can motivate you to make a change in your life; I will show you how life challenges can cause you to have more faith, and I will guide you in discovering how, when stepping deeper into that faith, you can step into your healed self. I will explain how once you begin to see your healed self as never having been wounded, you begin to walk deeper into the understanding that divine love and self-love are the ultimate truth.

When you open to love, you begin to realize you are not alone and the power that created you is there to support you, no matter what is going on in your life. I will share with you the answers that can be found in nature and how nature is here to comfort, love, and guide you on your path. When you realize all this, you see deeper into the consciousness of self and the collective, so you begin to understand deeper levels of love and happiness and how to be you authentically. Not only will your belief in yourself be stronger, but that belief will connect you deeper into the understanding behind the power of belief, teach you about living in the now, and help you develop your own principles to live by. I will explain the gift of patience on your journey and how it will serve you. Finally, we will touch on the business of healing and how to develop your strength as a leader.

Ultimately, writing this book has taught me to have faith in the power that created us and also to live with a sense of trust that we are always exactly where we need to be. It is my wish that it sooth your aching heart and worried mind and bring you into a place of contentment and ease. But I also hope it will help you see past your wounds and give you the strength and confidence to step into an empowered you.

The word leadership can be loosely tossed around and doesn't always go hand-in-hand with spiritual concepts, thoughts, beliefs, and practices. But to me, leadership begins with self-excellence. It is a cultivated art that starts with self. At the center of great leadership is the person who more than anything else makes a difference—YOU! And when you take a deep dive into self, you not only can be a better leader of self, but for others. I want to share with you a few tools that assisted me in gaining more self-confidence, more self-awareness, and more self-love. Oh, what I wouldn't give for you to know how deeply I appreciate you, not just for buying my book, but for your desire to step further into your Self because I believe, together, we have the power to change the world and make it a better place, especially when we shift together.

So it is with great love that I share my heart and my journey into self with you. I hope this book inspires you into your greatness! Thank you for sharing this lifetime with me, and even if no one else tells you this today—I appreciate and love you! I'm holding the space for your journey.

Are you ready to get started on stepping into your becoming? Are you ready to step out of your comfort zone? If so, good! Let's lock arms and begin this journey into developing the leadership principles for embracing change and achieving self-mastery!

Best Wishes,

Nicole Gabriel

PART 1

AWAKEN

Today, more people are awakening spiritually than ever before. We are longing for more than the material world. Many times we awaken through crisis. That crisis can be the loss of a loved one, a traumatic event, a personal or family illness, a job change, or a move. It can even be a positive crisis like a promotion, or come about through a general psychic opening that occurs within dreams or a kind of clairvoyant awareness. You may suddenly start feeling bothered by negative people or energies around you, have a desire to find yourself, or experience a sudden awareness of recurring life patterns. Or you may have unexplained panic attacks, an extreme sensitivity to electronics, deep dreams, or long periods of lost time or zoning out. You may notice changes in your sleeping habits or energy levels, experience periods of dizziness, weight gain or loss, or a need to detox the body. You may have cravings for certain types of foods, feel a stronger connection with nature, or notice a change in your preferred entertainment forms, topics of conversation, or personal interests. You may be asking yourself, "What is real? What is happening to my physical experience? What is the government doing for us? What is being hidden from us? Do institutions have our best interests in mind?" When you find yourself in this situation, do not be alarmed. You are just breaking away from the illusions and stepping into your awakened self. Even if you have been through a significant change, you might still be awakening to, transforming, and realizing your authentic self-truths in new ways as the onion layers peel away and unveil a new you.

AWAKEN — TRANSFORM — REALIZE

Chapter 1

Get On With It Already!

"As you start to walk out on the way, the way appears."

— Rumi

Are you tired of talking about your wounds, waiting for something great to happen that never does, or living in a continuous story of "I don't knows" or "only ifs"? Have you thought about your optimal self at a time far off in the future but not been able to see that person here and now? Have you realized that the time is now? Have you realized that your past experiences don't break you but only make you stronger?

Stepping into your becoming is not just a pie-eyed idea about what could be *some* day, but what can be here and now. Your becoming is in process right now as we speak. It is what you will be tomorrow based on what you do today. It's your authentic, powerful self. If you strive to be the best person you can be, then it starts today with a choice. The choice may be to let go of past wounds, but it might also be simply to own your essence, your true self. It may begin with the idea that, ultimately, God is the doer of everything and is holding you in every breath, but it continues with conscious choices on how to live your life. You get to decide what you believe in and what's important to you and, through your awareness and reflection of self and other, transformation occurs. But you might be also thinking that in order to make all these choices, you must begin by also making a change. Perhaps the changes have already been made for you and you're now picking up the pieces, or perhaps you are choosing to do something different. Either way, here we are. So let's start talking a bit more about what to do about it.

Coping with Change

Your wounds and past experiences have forever changed you; you will never be the same person you once were. The people in your life may never be the same either. Be it death, a job change, a divorce, or even sending your child off to college—nothing was ever meant to stay the same. The nature of our world is change. But how can you put your chin up and get on with life after devastating changes occur? How do you shake the emotions and break from being haunted by your past?

If you are asking these questions, then it is likely you are taking notice of the change(s) in your life already and seeking solutions. All change happens for a greater purpose than we are aware of at the time so it's a great idea to have faith in the greater plan. If you are like me—tired of talking about past wounds and ready to move on with a joyous life—then let's jump right in with what to do when change happens.

It can be challenging to move past coping and fighting the change, and to learn to adjust your thinking. But it's important not to deny the change or to try to run or hide from it. It's a good idea to face your feelings about the change in your life, especially when the change appears to be out of your control. Move yourself past being the victim and asking "Why me?" or "What did I do to deserve this?" Stop telling yourself, "It isn't fair." Figure out what your fears or worries are. This can take time and reflection. You don't have to be a victim even when you are not in control of the change that happened in your life. When dealing with change, it's important to realize it's a process. Below are a few tips about how to deal with change.

Strategies for Coping with Change:

1. Accept the change.
2. Reflect on changes you've coped with in your life that you've survived and thrived through.
3. Keep a journal.
4. Identify what can and cannot be controlled in the situation.
5. Take care of yourself with healthy new habits. Start new diet or exercise regimes.
6. Take it one day at a time.
7. Remind yourself of prior successes and don't let negativity affect your confidence.
8. Find a mentor. Seek help and support from others. It's a big world and many others have survived something similar. You are not alone.

9. Learn to be an optimist.
10. Change your vibration. (I will talk a bit more about this as we go.)

EXERCISE:

Begin noting your feelings and experiences in a journal. Writing is a great way to release your feelings, emotions, and thoughts; it is also a great way to reflect on your progress as you move through change. Write about your feelings. Reflect on what you are rejecting or accepting about the change and ask yourself, "What am I going to do about it?" Note your choices in your journal and reflect later on the shifts in your thinking. Make a list of your positive thoughts that build bridges to new possibilities and opportunities, and note your negative thoughts that block your ability to get there. Find ways to adapt to your new life and begin to welcome the change as a new opportunity. Keep a record of the choices you make and the attitudes and thoughts you have about them. Try to find ways to be grateful for the changes. Have you been freed after years of taking care of a sick loved one? Liberated from a dead-end job? Are you now available to meet the love of your life? To move? What about the change has made an improvement in your life?

Coping with Loss

I struggled with loss and the deaths of my loved ones. Losing a loved one can be a very traumatic time, and how you cope is a very personal experience. I knew all the losses and changes in my life were meant to be and had a purpose, but what was that purpose?

My hairy children (my Chinese Shar Pei dogs) have been among the most important relationships in my life. As I detailed in my earlier book, *Finding Your Inner Truth*, I experienced the loss of five of them in a row, an experience that I found devastating. I had to learn how to cope with this grief when other people could not seem to understand how the losses of "pets" could send me spiraling into such a dark place. At the end of that period, I found myself starting my new life in Maui, Hawaii with my fiance, Patrick, but Shiitake, my nearly six-year-old Chinese Shar Pei, had been diagnosed with lymphoma just ten days before I moved, so I spent every waking moment worrying about her and her care. She was my child, not my dog, and the only thing familiar about my new life in Maui was her presence. I also spent every last dollar I had to try to heal her, then begged people for more. The only new friends I made for the first eight months on Maui were those at the veterinary clinic. I was there at least once a week. Shiitake consumed my thoughts so much that I didn't want to plan a wedding or pretend I was enjoying what was supposed to be our island paradise. It was all I could do to go through the motions of existing and trying to make peace with God's plan to take my best friend from me.

I knew that Shiitake's death was a part of God's plan. I had just spent the last decade of my life journeying through spiritual teachings geared toward helping me with the most traumatic times of my life, so I was supposed to be in a better place of acceptance with it. I was certainly more educated about the process of death. After years of death and transformation, I had new tools and a new perspective. I fought the idea of another loss for me and a going home for her. I knew the steps to go through both physically and spiritually, but psychically, my senses went into their normal mode—opening up to everything!

In my human-ness, I was denying her passing, angry about it, and trying an all out bargaining campaign with God to keep her here. I was depressed for months about her sickness, especially since I saw myself as a powerful healer, and I thought I should have been able to help her. I had traveled the world learning healing techniques (working with Shaman healers all over Central America), but nothing I had learned worked for her. I even believed I had killed her because I gave her two rounds of rabies shots to move her to Hawaii; I feared that had triggered the onset of her lymphoma. I felt as if I had chosen Maui over her, which made it very hard to be on the island. However, my other dog, Sushi, had gone through the same vaccinations and was still with me, so that somewhat lifted the blame from my shoulders. But I still couldn't accept that it was Shiitake's time to leave, and I wondered what I could have done differently. She was not quite six years old, so I felt it was too early to lose her. I understood her life here was temporary, but couldn't the timing have been better?

Shiitake represented all that remained of my past back in Michigan, including my last attempt to heal my broken marriage before I met Patrick and moved west. She was the only constant amid the storm that was my life from 2006 until 2012. By comparison, twelve-year-old Sushi was no longer the same dog she was when younger; she no longer interacted with me the way Shiitake always had. Shiitake was the fourth pup to leave me during that period. I was not ready to let all of my past go with her, but I knew I had to. It was important for her (and for me) to move on. I needed to give her permission to go and give myself permission to heal. I was well overdue being ready to move into my present life.

After Shiitake left us, the house was cold and quiet. Sushi and I sulked around for months. Life had changed so drastically in the last few years. Shiitake was just one more death in a constant string of losses—death, divorce, family dramas, and sickness. Those losses had also led to a tremendous surprise—the life-changing opening of my psychic vision that resulted when I sought out spiritual avenues to help me heal from my pain. While it had led to some healing, it had also caused a lot of chaos in my life, and now Shiitake's death caused me to revisit many dark parts of myself.

Patrick saw that I was sad, but he told me how well I had handled her death and he reminded me that I had to have known I would outlive my dogs. He was being logical, but after so many years of loss and change, I felt too numb to move on. I had decided to live life, but I failed to see its purpose if so much loss were only going to continue. After the long spiritual journey I'd been through, as detailed in my previous book, *Finding Your Inner Truth,* I knew something was wrong because I had failed to see what I had gained. How could I celebrate any gain amid so much change and loss? I learned that loss was just a part of life, and in this change, so much can be learned. I grew thankful for her life. Can you do that for any of your losses? Can you become thankful?

Learning to Be Thankful for Loss

"The purpose of life is to watch and experience living.
To enjoy living every moment of it.
And to live in environments, which are calm,
quiet, slow, sophisticated, elegant. Just to be.
Whether you are naked or you have a golden robe on you,

that doesn't make any difference.
The ideal purpose of your life is that you are grateful—great and full—that you are alive, and you enjoy it."

— *Yogi Bhajan*

Something within me knew I needed to be thankful for the time I had spent with Shiitake. After all, it's a great big world, so many other souls could have come to me, but she was the one who had. She must have needed this short stay on earth to advance her soul. And I needed her to hold me together during the most trying times of my life so I could finally open my heart. She was the driving force that allowed me to complete my first book and push forward in my life.

Shiitake had been different from my other Shar Peis. I sensed that her soul had been more advanced than other dogs I had met. Her death taught me that souls do not leave us but become a greater part of us. As she initially began to pass, I could see her fear of the unknown. But as she left, she seemed to remember where she came from and where she was going. The moment she passed, I felt her become infused into the all that is (including me). I felt her move into peace and freedom. I felt her in my breath, in my arm, in my leg, in my consciousness—I was breathing and feeling her! I learned that she had left so that I could trust and know that the all that is is made up of our most trusted advisors and loved ones, as well as the ancients and the masters—all guiding us in the physical realm.

We are not really meant to die.
Our soul is immortal and we can never be destroyed.
The wave comes to the shore, and then goes back to the sea;

it is not lost.
It becomes one with the ocean,
or returns again in the form of another wave.
This body has come, and it will vanish;
but the soul essence within it will never cease to exist.
Nothing can terminate that eternal consciousness.

— *Paramahansa Yogananda*

We are all a part of a greater conscious intelligence that we return to when our time here on earth is done. Our spiritual essence is indestructible. Shiitake showed me that this consciousness is there to aid, help, and guide us. It's also there to welcome us back home. The change of her form didn't mean she was leaving me entirely; she was just changing her clothing and going back home to the astral world.

Upon her passing, Shiitake let me know she had served her purpose and was not meant to stay longer than she had. She was not meant to struggle though life in her physical body any longer. It would be a welcome rest. She showed me her wisdom and courage through her death. She had drifted into a peaceful place where the weighted body's pain no longer challenged her; there was no need to breathe oxygen, and only the joy of Spirit existed.

Once Shiitake was gone, I knew that I could not indulge my grief because it would only hold her back from where she needed to go. I knew this from the teachings of spiritual leaders, such as Paramahansa Yoganandya, who wrote:

> When a dear one dies, instead of grieving unreasonably, re-

> alize that he has gone on to a higher plane at the will of God, and that God knows what is best for him. Rejoice that he is free. Pray that your love and goodwill be messengers of encouragement to him on his forward path. This attitude is much more helpful. Of course, we would not be human if we did not miss loved ones; but in feeling lonesome for them we don't want selfish attachment to be the cause of keeping them earthbound. Extreme sorrow prevents a departed soul from going ahead toward greater peace and freedom.

Shiitake had shown me that we are *never* alone! I loved her and knew she loved me, and I knew I could trust what she was showing me in my consciousness. I knew she had to go so she could teach me. I saw that love is the only truth. I loved her enough to trust the truth she was showing me—that our love was endless. This was not the end, but simply the beginning.

I reminded myself that all the loss I had experienced was so that each being who left me could guide me. All my pups who had died before me became intertwined in my essence. Tia would lift my right leg, Mai Tai my left, Sangria my right arm, and Shiitake my left. I would serve my "term" here on earth, being led by my most trusted advisors. I was eternally grateful. Today, I am led and I trust because of those I have lost. I have learned that I am not here to walk this earth journey alone. I would never again take another step alone! I learned that where there is love, there is no fear, and where there is no fear there, there is no anger.

Shiitake taught me to have faith and be with the grace of God. She showed me I had a choice of what to do next, how to feel, how to consciously be. What losses or changes in your life have taught you that? I started to see that I could live as the best person I could be in honor of her if I could no longer do it for myself; then eventually, I began to do it myself. It was a day of true freedom when I began to take notice of that. Can you dedicate your being to someone else if you can't do it for you? It will shift you out of depression and you will begin to value your life even more as each day goes by. When you begin to value your life because someone else didn't get to keep his or her physical body, you begin to see how precious life is.

Where Is God?

I had been so angry when all the deaths had started occurring. I had hated God because I believed God hated me. But as time went on, I knew God had to love me more than words could express. I really thought about it and asked myself again how could God take Shiitake away from me? Then I paused. I realized God had given her to me to begin with.

If you are dealing with loss right now, ask yourself:

How can God take away ___ from me?

Who gave ____ to me?

Who can tell God what to do?

If God had created Shiitake and I had felt so much love from her, I could only imagine what love God had for me. God allowed her to show me this love, and I had experienced love and devotion from her like I had never experienced with another human. And while

God had overseen the experience for us, it was the connection between Shiitake and me, our mutual love and the trust, that ultimately showed me the infinite of which she was now a part.

I was shown that my soul's composition is the same as the collective consciousness Shiitake had shown me. If that collective was some kind of God, then God was within me, around me, and was/is me! Is it possible that "DOG" really is "GOD"? I think there is no way there can be separation! I have heard many yogic chants and speeches over the years claiming that God is not simply outside of us, but until Shiitake showed me, I had never confirmed this. We are all here temporarily, and then we go back to the consciousness that knows all. I began to wonder how the consciousness could be interacted with. Would I be able to call on it? Of course—because it was within me! Not only was it within me—it was me. I was not just the light of God, but I was the God light.

Shiitake was gone physically, but more present in every other way. I could see the spark of her soul with my psychic awareness. She taught me that the soul energy resides in the pineal gland (the place between the eyes at the root of the nose) here in our earth body. She showed me that this was how I would recognize her when she was without her physical body. It is like a golden ball of light of her essence. It is her recognizing factor when in spirit form. It's a unique calling card that we all have. It is how we recognize each other's spirit with or without the physical body. I loved her even more! I was thankful for what she was teaching me. Through her love and my trust, I would be the closest to God I had ever been at any moment. She was proving to me that spirit is strong in all sentient beings and no single one is more important or less important than another. Our life, just like our death, is purposeful. No one will ever convince me that she was just a "pet" because that would mean I had ownership over her. Her soul was grand in her physical body, but even more grand when it was no longer trapped in it. She was teaching me that we might have physical limitations, but our soul can be everything.

My curiosity to know more would be sparked and that curiosity would prove to be nearly enough to snap me out of the emotional wounds of my past and the emotional loss of her physical presence. What would snap you out of where you are now and move you into a more intentionally aware being? What would it take to move you from where you are to where you want to be? Is it one moment or several? Are you aware it is these moments that transform you? How can you place these transformation nuggets into your everyday awareness?

Tips For Stepping Into Your Becoming:

1. Let go and love.
2. Let go and let God.
3. Trust in the power of love.
4. When in doubt follow love.
5. Step out of your own way.
6. Talk to those you love who have departed; they will answer (in spirit and in the physical).

EXERCISE:

Make a list of all that you have lost—people and possessions. _____

How did each of these serve you in their lives and through their losses?

Have you given those you have lost permission to leave? If not, do so now. Cut all ties and allow each person to be free from your pain. Let each one go back home. Maybe create an altar or burn a candle in their honor for a period of time. Make notes here of this experience.

Can you find a way to be thankful for all things surrounding the loss? How can you make peace now with that loss? What do you need to do now to be thankful for the change in your life? What have you been freed up to do now? Can you live your life in honor of that loss?

What would being thankful look like if you could release the emotions of the loss?

AWAKEN — TRANSFORM — REALIZE

Chapter 2

What Now God?

"Fear ends where faith begins."

— Georgio A. Dano

Now that Shiitake had shown me I was not alone, I realized there was no need to be depressed. I had spent so much time trying to connect with those I had lost only to find now that they had never left me. When I began to run through the list of each being I had lost, I was overcome with love. I felt them come into me and fill my body, mind, and soul with love. I was infused with love and light. This seemed to heal me of the idea that I was just dropped here on earth to figure it all out and those I lost had deserted me. I no longer wanted to end my existence to be with those I lost, and I saw how silly that thinking was. But I began to wonder why I was put through so many trials if those in spirit who loved me were looking out for me. Why didn't they help? Then I thought, "Well, maybe they did since it could have been much worse than it was." Do you ever have those talks with God? The kind of talks where you wonder whether God is listening and why you don't get an immediate response? God had a plan, but not one that I expected.

Almost immediately after Shiitake died, I felt pretty low and did not understand everything she showed me or what to do about it. Many times during my spiritual transformation, I was able to interact with spirit in amazing ways, but many times I became confused about what this interaction was supposed to do for me. I would have profound visual experiences and interact with a world that most don't see. It felt as if I were a child in an imaginary world with invisible friends. But whatever it all meant, it was made clear to me that God was present within and around me in amazing ways, and I was transforming out of the old ways of my past and into my becoming.

Patrick and I decided a new addition might help heal my heart and soul and it was time to welcome a new pup into our home. I had sought out and found a potential breeder for a new pup and had one on reserve. The only problem was she hadn't been created yet. Her momma, whom we hadn't even met yet, was over on the island of Kauaii and wasn't even pregnant. And her daddy was still on the mainland.

I had to wait for her daddy to arrive, her momma to get pregnant, and eight more weeks for her birth before she could come into our lives. This was going to be a long wait—four to six months! But God had another plan and we found our bulldog Leilani. We went to look at her and knew right away she would join our family. Not only did she come home with us that day, but she became my constant companion. She slept at my feet, spooned me in my bed, and did daily meditation right at my ankles. She was helping to heal my heart. Eventually, I would fly over to the island of Kauai and Bella (short for

Portabella and named after my other mushroom—Shiitake) would come home with us, too. Bella and Leilani were quick to become the best of friends. But the breeder also knew I was interested in doing the only thing I hadn't in the twenty-five years I owned the breed—to have puppies! So, shortly after Bella came home, we welcomed Bella's boyfriend Blue Smoke (or "Bubba"). Now our house was filled with action, adventure, and love. My heart was still healing, and I was trying to communicate with Shiitake, but that was broken by the constant interruption of one, two, or three puppies. I still talked to Shiitake every day and slept with her picture beside me. I would wake to a bed full of puppies. Then I would look at those sweet little beings next to me and Shiitake's face in the picture and I would just cry. I felt so loved. I was beginning to feel a joy for life again like I hadn't for many years prior. But I also felt helpless in my ability to protect my new family. I was beginning to awaken out of my pain and the emotional wounds of my past. But just as I was getting strong again, God gave me a series of trials.

Have you ever asked God for answers and not liked the results? Did you wonder whether God misunderstood your request or prayer?

Don't Harm My Babies!

When Leilani came into our house, she brought ticks with her. Soon we were dealing with an incredible Hawaiian tick infestation! I had never seen anything like it. All these sweet little beings had ticks, and they were having severe allergic reactions. They were all red, swollen, and itchy. I felt so bad for them that my heart ached. I just would cry and cry. I tried every natural cure known to get them off the dogs and out of the house. I was losing my mind. The bite of one type of tick in particular caused dizziness similar to vertigo. Because Sushi was aging, the tick bites caused her to grow weaker. She was nearly deaf and blind now too. The pups also noticed she was growing weaker and began to harass her.

I always research any animal that repeatedly shows up in my life, so I found some fascinating information on what the tick is believed to symbolize. Much of what I found suggested someone or something might be "sucking the very life out of me," or in other words, "draining my energy." At this point, my graphic design business was becoming very busy, so it was very hard for me to keep up with it as well as the new pups, Patrick, and the need to keep healing my heart. My energy has always been sensitive, and people who don't know me well (and many who think they do) don't understand how much work I have to do to balance my energy. It's been this way my whole life. When God gives you something bigger than yourself, you do the best you can do and pray for a solution. When I could no longer find something that worked, I put my hands up in the air and gave it over to God. From my spiritual studies, I knew God to be the "doer of everything." It was time to give in and ask for help. Once I learned the ticks' message, they seemed to disappear almost overnight. Because I had changed my perception (mostly), I had changed the outcome. Fascinating!

Have you ever looked at a situation from a different perspective and shifted the outcome? Have you ever just stopped thinking so hard and just gave into the issue, only to find an amazing solution presented itself? How would you live differently knowing that the divine is holding you with every breath and every step you take? I began to step deeper into my faith because I didn't know what else to do.

Unfortunately, the tick infestation had already taken its toll on Sushi. I hoped she would pass naturally and peacefully, yet each morning, I gave a sigh of relief when I saw her breathing. I began wondering why God held onto her for so long when I could see she was not enjoying her life but struggling through her day. I had never needed to make such a decision before, but I realized I might have to consider helping her pass. I questioned whether I had the right to play God in this way, but I felt I owed it to her for being my constant companion for so many years.

She had come from a rescue situation that was quite sad, and only one of her littermates had survived after the rescue. The morning I was considering putting her to sleep, I was contacted by a woman who had been part of her rescue many years earlier. She told me Sushi's littermate had died two years ago at fourteen years of age. The woman was surprised to know one of the group was still alive. I had thought Sushi was twelve, but it turned out she was a whopping sixteen years old! This was Sushi's "ticket to ride." I couldn't watch her struggle any longer. I knew I needed to get strong for her. I wanted her to stay with me forever, but that wouldn't be fair to her. I had always heard, "They will let you know when it's time," and that morning she lay on my feet, which was something she had never done before and I took it as a sign she was ready to go home. Later that night, she would be buried next to her "sister" Shiitake, upcountry in Maui. Sushi would teach me just to let go and trust in a power greater than me because this is only a temporary place for our spirit. On earth, the spirit works hard, but she always showed me how to reflect and take time out just to enjoy quiet moments.

After Sushi's death, our home was filled with an incredible kind of peace I had not known following the passing of my other four babies. The peacefulness that came over our home was fitting with her presence (whether physical or in spirit). She had a way of holding space. Her spirit didn't hang around and never even came for a visit. I believe she was celebrating after the many years of separation from her soul's true home. Her passing was much easier on me because I knew she had lived a long and full life, but so much of my past was wrapped up in her little brown package. Her passing finally forced me to say goodbye to all that was my past. My heart now belongs to Maui, and Shiitake and Sushi will forever sit on a Haleakala mountainside under a little tree covered in a soothing orange moss, marked by two gravestones engraved with their pictures and names, adorned with flowers and a few dog toys. Each day when I wake, I look out the back window and know they are up high looking down upon me, and each day I am reminded that we are not permanent here and to breathe is a gift. Nothing around us is permanent. Everything moves on. This is the Spirit of the Universe.

What (or who) are you attached to that you could release from? Did you know that if you release from them now in the physical, it becomes less painful to release from them in spirit? It becomes easier to allow them to live according to their own free will and in accordance with God's divine plan. I believe Sushi's passing showed me how to free both of our souls to live without being held back in any way. If you've lost loved ones, or they are still present with you, it is very important to detach emotionally, but don't confuse detachment with non-love. In my opinion, to really love people is to set them free to be all that they can be without constraints of any kind. Imagine cutting cords all around your self and your loved one with a big pair of imaginary scissors. Feel the freedom. This freedom will allow them and you to step into a more empowered self, even in the most trying of times.

It is important to remember that God has a plan. You wrote that plan with God before you came here. Each soul has something it needs to experience, and no matter what that is, you must free the individual soul to live out that plan. It can hurt sometimes to watch, and you can place blame on self or others, but with the next story, I am about to share, you will see that sometimes there is nothing you can do but give in to that plan and allow.

Rescuing Bella

The pups were old enough now to go on some pretty amazing hikes around the island. As Patrick and I and the pups took these walks, I would think about how this new life was going to be so much better. It was time to focus on all the gifts I had here on Maui. The land was beautiful and healing. We were hiking regularly. We had a regular schedule and location.

One day we had hiked a ways and were resting at our regular bench overlooking the scenery. All of a sudden, I looked around and didn't see Bella. Where was she? My heart sank! There was only one place she could have gone—over a three-hundred-foot, eighty-degree-incline cliff!

Oh my God! Oh my God! Oh my God! I nearly jumped over after her! We couldn't see her, but now we could hear her crying, yelping. The other dogs were trying to get over the edge to get to her, which nearly resulted in our losing Blue as well. The closer Patrick and I got to her, the closer the other dogs got, too. Patrick held them back while I tried everything I could to get to her, but I couldn't see her.

My body started to shake. All we could see were the high grasses and ferns on the cliffside, but we assumed she was holding on and possibly sliding farther down with every breath or each movement. We had no idea how much longer we had to reach her before she slid all the way down. I was completely exhausted and distraught. I had no other choice but to call the fire department to see whether they could rescue her. I felt my body seize up and my heart pump. I was in a state of shock. It was getting dark and there was nothing else we could do to reach her.

Once I made my phone call, the fire department and animal control explained that it was unlikely they could do anything either. I couldn't believe they weren't prepared for a situation like this since the landscape was so full of cliffs I would have thought such situations were a regular occurrence. I thought I just hadn't called the right person. In a panic, I began calling everyone I thought might remotely be able to help.

I watched Patrick stand there, making no attempts to get to her. He was holding the other dogs back, but he had no suggestions to rescue Bella. I know he was keeping the other dogs safe, but I thought he was my hero. He was supposed to save her. I couldn't understand why he wasn't as panicked as I was. Part of me was angry about that. But why was I taking all this out on Patrick? He didn't deserve to be treated this way (even if it were just in my thoughts). He really didn't have any other skills than I did, so I don't know what I expected him to do. I knew we would likely both die if we tried to rescue her ourselves, but if one of us didn't, so would she.

I was screaming internally at God, asking "Why is this happening to me? What did I do to deserve this kind of pain?" I had already survived so much loss, and now this. What was I supposed to do? Why was God giving me something larger than me that I had no control over? Why was no one helping? Why was God testing me in such a painful way?

After several hours, the fire department surprisingly called me back and told me to come down and meet them at the base of the mountain to guide them up to where Bella was. I was so relieved that we were going to scoop her up off that cliff in a heroic effort led by trained professionals and take her home that night! I went hiking down to meet them.

They geared up and we all hiked back up to the cliff. But when they got there, they could not see her. She was crying and yelping, but they told us they were instructed not to put their lives in danger to rescue a dog. They also stated that if it had been a human they would have stayed all night! I couldn't believe someone would make a call on the importance of one soul over another! I nearly flipped! I was not thinking clearly and just wanted my baby rescued. My mind was racing with how to make that happen, but I think I was taking out my anger with God—through my thoughts (not words)—on those who were there but unable to save her.

How could I begin to convey to an entire fire department that animals have souls and are angels sent to teach us—and do it before the sun went down? There was no way! They'd simply think I was crazy…or at least irresponsible for letting Bella get into this situation to begin with. I knew they'd keep trying if they understood, but instead, they didn't try at all. No one went to get her. They told me they were instructed to call the rescue off. They would have to leave her in the dark over night and try again in the morning.

I was losing my mind! How could she survive? What could I do? My mind was racing. I thought maybe I could go home and build something to get down there to get her. Maybe I could do…what? I was not an experienced climber! I was not strong enough to get down there and get her back up. And if I got down there, how would I get back up? Well, I certainly wasn't leaving her! I would just stay all night with her then.

Then the firemen told me they would have to escort us out! I gasped! Not only could they not save Bella, but she had to be left alone in the dark all night by herself. There was absolutely nothing I could do! My body was in a state between numb and sick. I could barely move. Then all my muscles tightened and I fell to my knees. I was supposed to be her guardian! How could I have let this happen?

I knew that if I left Bella that night, I might never see her alive again. I called down to her and told her she was a good girl, and that Mommy loved her. And I told her I was so, so, so sorry and that I would be back to rescue her in the morning.

I couldn't imagine how I'd ever get over what I had done to her! I left her unsupervised and she had gone over the side. She was just a baby! She was only six months old! How could I live with this? She was scheduled to have eye surgery in two days so she could see better. I couldn't believe she'd never make that appointment. I was just sick.

The firefighters told us to lower a shirt down to her. They said our scent might keep her in one spot all night. Patrick took off his shirt and tied it to the end of a leash. We tied three leashes together, lowered them down, and hoped they were long enough to reach her and the idea would work. The other dogs were there with us the whole time. We had to watch them as we gave up their leashes.

The firefighters then grabbed our arms at the elbows, saying they had to escort us off the trail. My knees didn't bend and I couldn't make my legs walk. Patrick pulled me. Then I just lost it and sobbed like a baby the entire way down. I had so much pain in my body. My heart felt like it was going to stop beating and my legs felt like lead weights.

When we got to the bottom, it felt as if we had walked for days. We put the two dogs in the car and Patrick took the driver's seat. We talked with the firefighters, who told us they would be out there at dawn to try again. They said there might be a chance for a helicopter rescue if she were still alive and barking in the morning. Again, I gasped. As we drove away I felt a kind of energetic elastic band stretching between Bella and me. It stretched until it could stretch no more as we separated farther from each other. It felt as if she were an entire universe away.

When we got home, Patrick brushed his teeth and got in bed. How could he be so relaxed? I didn't have human kids and one of my three babies was out in the dark on a ledge facing her death! It was past her bedtime, and we were all snuggled in bed without her. She represented the new hope for my future. I had hoped that one day I would breed her and she would become a momma. It had been my dream to have baby pups since I could remember. It now seemed like Bella represented all my hope for a new life and a new start. I thought: *How can God be so unfair as to make her suffer? Why is God doing this to me after all the loss I've already been through? What do I still need to learn? What is this teaching me?*

I wanted to design something to rescue Bella with. I felt that going to bed was a useless effort, but my brain couldn't come up with the right kind of contraption and nothing on my body was working. I couldn't think. I was shaking like a leaf. My knees hurt and wouldn't bend. The shaking was overwhelming my body. Patrick kept coaxing me to get in bed. I kept pacing. I thought that if I could quiet myself, I could talk to her, call the angels, or pray, but I was so exhausted. I tried to quiet myself by getting into bed, but by then, all my close spiritual and healer friends were contacting me and praying with me. My mom was up all night praying with me. We all tried to talk to Bella, to balance her energy, to call her spirit guides and angels and to talk to the spirits of the land. I used every technique I had been trained in during my spiritual sabbatical from life. I did each technique twice! My mom told me to try to rest—she would take over trying to talk to Bella. I was in tears because my mom was trying to help me like she had when I was a small child. We were both in profuse tears.

I put on my yoga music to try to relax my soul like I often did during the most trying times of my life. Snatam Kaur's words reminded me that God is within me, that the breath is life, and that God is a teacher and friend. I knew God would prevail and a great lesson was to be learned. My mom put on Snatam Kaur's music, too. It was almost as if we joined in a sacred circle.

Although I was exhausted and at times had to jerk myself back awake when I started to doze, I never prayed so hard in my life for the safety and care of another being! I called on Shiitake and asked her to call all of our spiritual family to help. I called on my deceased grandparents. I called on my angels and guides. I had deep talks with God. I told God, "This is not about me as much as it is about Bella." I told God, "Bella has such a full life to live here and so much more to do."

I realized that if Bella lived through this experience, I would never question my faith again! The gift of this miracle would forever move me. As I prayed, I kept finding myself jumping out of my sleep, hearing her yelp and seeing her fall. I wondered why I created this image in my head. Then I emotionally lost it and started deeply crying again.

I woke Patrick up. He told me I woke him from a dream where Jesus came to tell him Bella would be safe, and we'd see her in the morning. I wondered whether Patrick had more faith than I did. I cried and cried and cried. I was so exhausted that I couldn't sleep. I was comforted by Patrick's visions, but I wanted to get showered and dressed and get back out there with Bella. We had a plan that we would hike in from the bottom if they couldn't rescue her from the top, so we needed to prepare to go through the thick undergrowth and the heat of the sun to get to her.

I wondered what was going on in Bella's mind. What did her visions and thoughts look like? I told myself this situation might be like a

Native American Vision Quest that she needed to experience and triumph over for her own growth. I once had a friend who hung from his nipples for several nights in the dark woods with no food or water in a spiritual Native American Sun Dance ceremony, so how was this any different? Maybe there was some kind of soul pattern within Bella that needed this experience? If she survived it, then maybe I could accept it. And if she survived, I would also know her great strength. I would see, even more than I already had, that her life was purposeful and intentional. But would she survive?

I watched every single tick of the clock. I got up and paced the floor. It was still dark, but if I could have reached down under that sun somehow, I would have pulled it up. I would have.

Finally, we were driving back to meet the fire department crew. We were locked out at the gate, so we worried that they had been called out on another emergency. They told us that any human emergency would come before any attempts to rescue Bella. Then when they showed up in that big yellow truck, it scared me. I was so scared that Bella wouldn't bark. I talked to her all night, telling her she just had to get through a few more hours, and whatever she did, she had to bark when we called her.

When we got to where we could hike in, all of a sudden, my legs wouldn't go. I stood there shaking so badly that I couldn't talk or move. I believe my body was going into some kind of shock. The firemen had to drive me up the big hill because I couldn't walk. But then, all of a sudden, the hike in started. Patrick had gone in ahead of us. I walked as fast as I could, but my body just wasn't working. I was out of breath, and it was still dark. I kept tripping over my own feet. I thought I'd catch up to Patrick, but he stayed just ahead of me. I heard him call out for Bella, and I listened like a hawk for her reply.

Oh my God! God is so, so, so, so good! *She barked!* I fell over on the trail and started crying. I was yelling, "*She barked! She made it! She's alive!*" I yelled so loud that she started barking back at me. When I finally reached her, I was in tears. But what I hadn't realized was that the firemen hadn't brought their gear to get her. Why hadn't they geared up? What was happening?

Then they told us the chief himself was hiking up and had approved a helicopter rescue. As it turned out, he had been called about the rescue effort when he was at a wedding with his wife the night before. He and his wife were dog people, and she had told him that if it were their dog, she sure as hell would have had him out there rescuing it, whatever effort it took. God (and the chief's wife) were on our side!

It seemed like the entire day had gone by, but the chopper still wasn't there. I kept talking to Bella. They told us they were not sure they could rescue her. We had now waited for fourteen hours since she had first fallen, and we still weren't sure she would be rescued. First, they needed to do a fly by, and if they could see her, they could rescue her. I knew the helicopter might scare her, so I tried to paint for her a picture in my head (and convey it to her) of the helicopter. I tried to tell her it would be loud. I asked Shiitake to be there in spirit with her and comfort her.

Finally, after nearly fifteen hours, we had confirmation that the helicopter was en route to do its first fly by. It was a bright yellow bird, and as it approached, it was so loud. I could only imagine how tired and scared Bella was at that point. We were all motioning toward where she was, but just as quick as the helicopter came, it was gone. My heart sank. I thought Bella had fallen off or they couldn't see her, but as the helicopter went by, I talked to her and I could hear her barking back. I thought, *Oh God, they can't see her and they're giving up…after all this waiting!*

The chief was talking with the helicopter crew over the radio. He told us they were going to attempt the rescue, but someone had to come down to meet them after they got her down. Oh, dear God, after all this time, I couldn't imagine not being there to see her get into the arms of her rescuer.

I left Patrick on top of the hill, telling him to keep whistling to Bella and telling her she was a good girl. I ran down as fast as my legs would go. I stopped for a minute when I saw the yellow chopper through the trees. There was a man hanging from it in a rescue basket and I watched it circle around and approach Bella. It was just about there. I wanted to see the rescue to make sure they had her, but literally thirty seconds after they got there, they flew away. I couldn't see much through the trees. I thought the worst. I thought they scared her or dropped her. There was just no way they could scoop her up that quickly. I just stopped. I thought, *Oh God…do I run back up, or do I run down?* I decided I would be optimistic. Perhaps they just needed to approach again. I started to go down the mountain, but my knees seized up so I could barely walk. I had been up and down this mountain, two miles in either direction, four times. My legs moved as quickly as possible, but when I reached the bottom, the helicopter was gone. I swallowed my heart! I thought for sure it had dropped her.

Then I saw a group of men. The helicopter must have dropped off the rescuers? I walked sheepishly, unsure of what the crew would tell me. Even though I was looking right at Bella, I didn't see her. When I realized it was her, I didn't know how to react. She and I were both shocked! We were both unsure of what had happened. I approached her slowly, afraid she was an illusion. She was under the arms of her rescuer. Four guys were just hanging out there, talking and laughing. When I realized it was her, I grabbed her, holding her tightly and crying!

I asked the rescue crew to describe the scene since I had wondered all night how she could survive. They told me that on the entire mountainside, there was only *one* small ledge. It was not only just big enough for her to land on, but it was also the only spot clearly visible in the lush Hawaiian fern growth that surrounded her!

After hearing that, I had no doubt in my mind that a miracle of great proportions had occurred. I had no doubt that God loves me! I will never doubt that ever again as long as I live! Bella is an absolute miracle! Every day when I look at her, I can't help but think of those sixteen hours. Now we fondly call her "Mirabella"—the miracle dog!

It would be this one event that would truly shift things for me. When nothing makes sense but turns out in your favor, it's nothing short of a miracle. I can't fully understand what happened in those fifteen hours, but I do know that something magical happened. Have you had one event that you can thank for shifting you into a different place?

Because of this event, not only am I now more aware of miracles, but I know that the source that created me places everything in my life for a specific purpose because I am strong enough to handle it. Begging for

Bella's life to be spared had me asking questions about why life was so important; it shifted me into a place of asking how I would consciously choose to live this one physical life that I have been given. In some regard, it would also confirm that I knew nothing. But what it did confirm is that I—we—are responsible for our own actions and responses. If I truly had faith in the power that created me during this event, I might have been more calm and understood that everything happening was exactly perfect as it was. I would have had faith. But I also know that everything did happen exactly as it should have because now I have a new view on life, death, faith, and the choices I make with all of it going forward. I am thankful for the lessons taught to me over those fifteen-plus hours. And they keep teaching me.

Nearly eight months after this event, I woke myself up in a panic and realized that this incident with Bella had happened nearly one year, to the day and even time, after Shiitake's death. The night Bella spent on that cliff was the same night a year after Shiitake was profusely vomiting and preparing for her morning passing. At the time Bella was being rescued, Shittake was passing over the rainbow bridge. In my shamanic studies, this parallel would indicate a kind of pattern that needed to be "adjusted." As this realization became clear, I saw ethereal cords connecting the two pups together. I imagined cutting these to break the tie.

I also imagined cutting the cords because they related to traumatic events in my life. I began to cry profusely. My healer bulldog Leilani took notice and came thundering over to me; since I was still lying in bed, she stood on top of my heart, pressing exactly where it hurt. Her aura turned bright green. The color of a healer. I began to gift her back healing energy, and a circular kind of energy flow took place between us. I began to see that animals touch us always where energy needs to shift. Their motions are intended. They know exactly what to do to lift our spirits and heal our hearts. So this miracle of Bella's would continue to teach well after it occurred.

Believing in Miracles

A miracle is defined as an event not explicable by natural or scientific laws. Such an event may be attributed to a supernatural being (God or gods), a miracle worker, a saint, or a religious leader. A miracle is an event which the forces of nature—including the natural powers of man—cannot produce by themselves, but requires the interference of a supernatural agency.

Miracles happen every day. When you change your perception of what a miracle is, you will see them all around you. When a miracle happens, it changes your perception of life and how the world functions. Bella's miracle made me see that God really does love me and always will. God loves all of us and always will. I know that God doesn't make mistakes. Miracles are like little expressions of love from the divine, and I am a believer because of them. Any time I question God's love for me, I tear up because I am so thankful for the lesson taught through Bella. Her life was spared, and only a miracle could have made it so. Her rescue was a miracle cure for any doubt I felt about God's love. Prayer is talking to God, but meditation is letting God talk to you. I prayed all night, knowing if I could bring myself into meditation the night Bella was on that cliff, I could hear God. My emotions fought me in and out of attempted meditation. As much as possible that night, I sat with love in my heart and full of faith. A prayer will go where it will, but when the heart goes into the prayer, every beat of the heart creates a miracle.

"I do not believe in miracles,
I rely on them."

— Yogi Bhajan

Overcoming Doubt

Has doubt paralyzed you? Do you doubt your knowledge, choices, instincts, or physical abilities? Are you worried you will be wrong? Maybe you've heard the saying, "The only wrong choice is not making one." What I've been learning is there is no such thing as making a wrong choice. One thing I took notice of during the most trying times of my life was that I doubted my abilities and didn't trust in myself. I became paralyzed. Doubts are an inevitable part of human life, but in my experience, doubt is the absence of God. Fear exists in doubt, and anger exists in fear. How do you find the hope that makes you act, rather than the fear that leads to conflict? Here are some tips that allowed me to move past doubt during the most trying times in my life:

1. "It's not the life that matters, it's the courage that you bring to it." (Yogi Bhajan)
2. You are not your fear.
3. Change your attitude about failure, and kill doubt with kindness. Let go of negative self-criticisms.
4. Set reasonable goals.
5. Set something in motion and be guided. It's easier to be guided when you are moving than when you are stationary and para-

lyzed in fear.

6. Build your confidence by seeing your success happen.
7. Make your choices with heart and compassion.
8. Expect nothing in return.

Yoga is a great tool to release doubt. I would often go into a yoga class thinking about all the things I was worried I might not be able to do or how I wasn't going to be able to keep up. But once the class was over, I would realize that the universe was conspiring at every moment to give me exactly what I needed. I have grand visions of how things are going to go in my life. Sometimes they work the way I suspect they will, and sometimes God has another plan. For example, I knew I needed to leave Michigan, but I never imagined I'd end up living in Hawaii. I have been learning that in order to meet a challenge spontaneously you have to develop your intuition to match the need. When I step into the role of yoga teacher in my life, and not just in the classroom, I become a path to elevation for myself and others.

"Do you have a practice, in collaboration
with your mind and consciousness,
that you shall not take revenge and you shall not have fear?"

— Yogi Bhajan

Yogi Bhajan, who brought Kundalini yoga to the West from India, said to have a conflict is a conscious act. But to keep it inside, and hidden, is a personal crime, and the moment you are afraid, you have forgotten there is a God, and that there is a guru inside you. Check your mind: Listen to what it is saying, what you are saying, and what your inner self/inner being is saying. These are three voices speaking at the same moment. First, separate them. When a thought comes, ask, "Who's saying what to me? What is the origin of this thought?" Most of the time, instead of doing that, the thought comes and you start recycling it. What a waste of your most precious life. Do you know why? Because the conflict is between you and your mind. But when you believe or know or feel, rightly or wrongly, that the ecstasy of God is with you, then your mind will behave, and your identity will not let you down. Then you will feel the guru within you. Then "God is in every part of me" will be felt. This can't be wrong! Nobody is without God. If you cannot see God in all, you cannot see God at all.

"Every disability is imagined.
Every achievement an experience.
Develop your courage to overcome
your imagined disability."

— Yogi Bhajan

Yogi Bhajan believed that inner conflict comes to us because we have the power given by God to solve it. We were born spiritual people with awakened souls. Fear and vengeance are habits, and we have to change them. Conflicts come to test your purity and piety, your union with God, your grace, and your reaction to conflict. Conflicts are a part of life. They are just like changing the sheets on the bed after you sleep in it.

Tips for Stepping into Your Becoming:

1. Know that God created you and will not intentionally harm you or your loved ones.

2. Trust in the power that created you.
3. Understand that God has a better plan than you can imagine.
4. Believe in miracles.
5. You have the power to conquer doubt. Use it.

AWAKEN — TRANSFORM — REALIZE

Chapter 3

Meeting the Hawaiian Gods

"'A'ohe pau ka 'ike i ka halau ho'okahi."
("All knowledge is not taught in one school")

— Hawaiian Proverb

After Bella's incident, I was forever changed. I connected more deeply to the land and began to understand the ways it (and Bella and me) was protected by the Hawaiian Gods. Upon further reflection, I began to understand what I was being taught. This episode with Bella had me thinking back to a time when Shiitake was ill and I had used all my tricks and tools to perform a healing ceremony on her. At the time, Patrick was traveling on the mainland, so I saw it as an incredible opportunity for me to try one last ditch effort to release her lymphoma. I knew I was a powerful healer. I was going to pull out everything I knew to perform what I envisioned to be the ceremony to end all ceremonies. That attitude was not necessarily the way to go into it, but my ego got the best of me...and the Hawaiian Gods had their way with me, too.

Healer with An Ego

A "healer" doesn't actually provide the healing…but the pathway for the healing to take place. It doesn't matter what kind of healing you're talking about, the concept is the same. I don't need to know what is wrong to deliver an effective healing. I am, after all, not the healer. I am merely a vessel for healing to occur. I used to teach my shamanic healing students to get out of the way and drop their attachments to get the best outcome from a healing. I can teach anyone how to do a healing. I cannot, however, teach someone to drop their ego…um… including myself, apparently.

I'm a very intuitive and visional person, but I am still human after all. I'm not always good at listening or following directions. I decided to get out a sacred Peruvian cloth called a mestana. In my shamanic training, this was used to tie together all of our sacred healing medicine tools to create what is called a mesa. The mesa is our medicine bag or bundle. It is said that the mesa or mestana can be laid open to create a kind of timeless portal that all light beings can travel through. The belief is that all previous healers of the lineage can come through to help out in the healing. I had a new mestana cloth I was going to make into a new medicine bag one day, but had not done so. I knew it to be a very powerful cloth based on prior healing work. I laid the mestana and the cloth down and opened the medicine bag on the ground in the garage. Then I prepared to do my healing ceremony for Shiitake.

I chose the garage as my healing location because I knew that everything I was lighting would stink up the house, and Patrick would smell what I was up to while he was gone. My "closet shaman" behavior would then be out of the bag. Patrick has never participated in my healing events or ceremonies, and when we first met, he was quite judgmental and unsure about them, so I had never put him through the classes or any such related events or practices. Because he is a Christian, he struggles with some of the concepts, but overall, he supports and loves me, and he knows I operate from a place of love. But these differences have placed challenges on our relationship in the past, so after many years, I have learned that it is sometimes best to keep all sacred matters sacred for self. After all, it's generally only me who has my own personal experiences. I have often wished I could be open and share everything with my partner, but Patrick simply doesn't take the time to devote to such matters. He is curious, but he is much more focused on his business and holds different beliefs. Part of my journey is honoring his.

Once in the garage, I started the ad hoc healing ceremony and lit white candles, sage, incense, sandal, and palo santo wood. I created a sacred space by calling in all the linear directions as I had been taught to do in my Peruvian Shamanic training—south (the serpent), west (the jaguar), north (the ancestors), east (the condor), pacha mama (down to the earth), and the apus (up to the gods of the mountains). The sun began to set so the garage grew dark, other than for the candle light. Shiitake looked up at me with her all knowing, magical golden eyes as if to say, "Are you sure, Mom?" Her eyes were deep windows to her soul, and everyone who looked into them would notice they were not just "dog eyes." I told her that Momma loved her, and if there were anything at all that I could do to heal her, I would do it.

I envisioned her body filling with light and healing. I danced and sang with a rattle in my hand. The garage was full of smoke. I was suddenly overtaken by a very forceful spiritual presence that scared both her and Sushi right out of the garage. I was curious about this presence and acknowledged it, but I continued rattling, dancing, and singing. I immediately sensed a very strong Hawaiian God was standing with me. He was not very welcoming, so I spoke intuitively with him, saying, "I am sorry I don't know your customary ways of healing, so please step aside and allow me to continue." I got a strong sense that I was *not* supposed to continue, but I did anyway. This was not about me, right? Right? This was for Shiitake. No! I was wrong! The whole ceremony was all about me. The presence told me not to do it, but I kept going. I was then told she would not survive. I argued, "Yes, she will survive." I had a dialogue with this being and an internal dialogue with myself. I kept dancing and rattling and began crying my eyes out at the same time. "Why can't I save her?" I yelled internally. "Is there nothing I can do? I will save her!"

My ego got the best of me. I thought the Hawaiian God was watching and learning from me like I was some kind of powerful healer who was going to show him how it was done. But all of a sudden, I felt this sickness in my stomach. I felt like I was going to throw up. The room started to warp and spin. I felt a surge of energy come through my feet into my body and then leave through my head. I was standing on the medicine cloth, and whatever was going through that portal was coming through me. It was *not* good! All of a sudden, one of the candles tipped over and the others blew out. Wax went everywhere. I kept going. My ego got in the way again. I thought I was shifting something and making a difference. Finally, I was drained emotionally and psychically, so I just stopped. Later that night, and for the next four days, I was sicker than I remember being in a long time. I had it coming out both ends. I had clearly done something, but it didn't appear to be related to Shiitake at all. This whole thing was about me. I needed to realize she was passing, and I needed to let her go. Her earth time was done. Despite all the countless attempts I had made, I was not going to keep my best friend alive. I was trying to direct the healing, not allow it. We essentially are assuming we know better than God, Spirit, Source, or the Universe when we try to direct the healing. I was getting in the way of what Shiitake really needed. I was actually not only doing myself a disservice, but her, too.

I so badly wanted to see the results of this healing in my favor that I became tied to the outcome. It is normal to want to see people heal through your efforts, but at some point, we must learn that we can't heal everyone. We are also not meant to change another's path. Shiitake's path was not meant to be changed that day, but I was meant to learn to let go.

Many things factor into a healing. We do not actually provide the healing; people must also be willing to heal. They must co-create and participate in their healing, and generally, they learn they have the power to heal themselves. I hate to say it, but some people don't really want to be healed. They might think they want to heal, they might say they do, but on a deeper level, it isn't always true. Sometimes a person becomes so attached to the story of his or her illness and the attention received by telling the story of that illness that the illness actually becomes the person's identity. We don't know what anyone's life path or destiny is meant to be, so we must detach from the outcome. We cannot play God; we *can* simply allow God to come through.

With both Shiitake and now Bella's events, I was in face-to-face combat with the ways of the Hawaiian ancestors. It wasn't that these beings didn't want to see a spontaneous healing occur, but what they were trying to tell me was that I was messing with something that was not meant to shift. I needed to come into agreement with the path of Shiitake's life...and death. They were telling me that she wasn't meant to stay, but I kept trying to "fix" something that wasn't broken. I never intended to disrespect anyone or anything. I just wanted to save Shiitake, but she was not meant to be "saved." I was also being taught in not so graceful terms to respect the ways of the ancients. I had learned about the proper protocols to work with spirit in ceremony in my initial shamanic classes, but I forgot about them as I approached this event. I allowed my emotions to get the best of me and didn't get out of the way. Instead, I tried to manipulate the healing for the outcome I desired.

After Bella's event, I had no choice but to be in more peaceful relationship with the gods of the land. I had been given two very strong lessons. I was taught to respect the ways of the Hawaiian culture. I knew there was much more to learn, though. I knew this was part of my journey being on Maui. I was once told by a shaman healer in Peru that I would become a great shaman. When I asked how, I was told "through experience" and "through life." Due to the language barrier, I couldn't ask too much more, but I had already been through a lot at that point and was a bit worried about what else was to come. I knew I was to teach myself, but I was always hopeful for a few guidelines, teachers, or gurus to appear as well. It seemed that once I knew the basics, I always knew how to run with it (with the exception of letting my heart get in my way with Shiitake's "forced" healing). I was hopeful Spirit would lead me to someone who could one day guide me into the ways of the Hawaiian healing methods, but I also knew, based on my past, I would need to learn on my own. I've learned over time that if there is something I am waiting for in another it generally means it's something I'm supposed to learn or master for myself.

Hopefully, my story will show you it's best not to get in your own way, and, whether you are a healer or not, allow God to come in and guide you. God created you, and God will bring you who and what you need with better clarity as the timing is appropriate. When you feel God is not supporting you and giving you what you need, you might want to check with your ego. If you feel drawn to know, learn, or change something and God doesn't send you a person, then God has confidence in you finding your own way. When beings come and go in your life, sometimes they are just meant to lead you down the path necessary to set the direction for your next stage of life.

Meeting Kahu 'Imai'kalani

Some time had now gone by since Shiitake's passing and Bella's rescue. I had been introduced to a Hawaiian man some months prior and was now visiting him on Oahu because he was going to take me to an ancient Hawaiian healing sight called a "heiau." He was going to connect me to the ancestors and show me the basics of doing a proper healing; I knew he would get me started in the right direction and confirm my visions or experiences in some way.

Our time together was short. We drove up a street, through a residential neighborhood to a location that seemed almost masked to hide itself from the more modern residential setting. Dark lava stones surrounded the land like a fence or border. The trees were old and overgrown. I could sense a dark and heavy presence here, which was a bit surprising to me considering it was a place of healing and refuge. It seemed like a place to leave your wounds. My guide would later explain that people came here to ask for healing. I didn't like the heavy feeling and didn't feel like I had anything that heavy to release. I was even a bit alarmed by the energetic density there. I had brought gifts with me to thank and honor the gods for teaching me and keeping Bella safe. The man briefly explained the process for entering the space. I knew he was watching to see how I approached the ceremony, my vision, and intuition…how connected I was. Perhaps the ancestors told him to watch out for me because I was recently caught by them in my ego, but I hoped those days were long behind me.

He told me his Hawaiian name, "Kahu 'Imai'kalani," and then he said he was going to call to the ancestors of the land with song to ask for permission to enter. He told me I would need to state my name when he motioned for me to do so. He suggested I use my spiritual name as given to me in the Kundalini yoga tradition—Nirankar Kaur (which means "one who sees God in all"). After receiving permission from the ancestors, he motioned that it was now okay to enter. I was relieved I wasn't kicked out because of my earlier antics. He gave me a bit of a tour and showed me where to leave my offerings, but he said I didn't have to leave them where everyone else did. It didn't feel right to leave them there, so I walked until I found the right place. I simply wanted to say thank you and leave, but then I was suddenly overcome by a need to open my medicine bag and leave something that represented my past. I suddenly didn't recognize who this person was who owned this medicine bag. I couldn't relate. I was clearly no longer this person. In fact, I was practically dumping things out of my bag. These items were once extremely sacred to me, so every time I traveled, they went with me (despite a few airport security issues); when I slept, they sat on the nightstand beside me, and whenever an issue presented itself, I reached for my healer's bag. I had been taught to blow my issues into it and release them from my "soul's blueprint" with the breath. On countless occasions, I reached for this bag like a life preserver until I was nearly dependent upon it. And here I was completely not relating to it. I realized I had made huge shifts in my life, so I was no longer this person with all these wounds. If it weren't for the expense of some of the items, I might have just left behind the whole thing.

I returned to the entrance, thanked all the ancestors, and then just started to tear up. Kahu 'Imai'kalani closed the healing session with another prayer, and then we talked for a few minutes. He told me I had been at the entrance of where it was said the gods lived. I sensed that. I felt I was in the presence of many ancestors. I sensed three or four very tall, spiritual beings who seemed to be shuffling about in what looked much like a "medicine kitchen." They were busy creating and overseeing the space, but they also felt very connected to another dimension, time, and place—perhaps they were interdimensional beings. I felt much heavy, sad energy around me. Before I knew it, I was crying over my ex-husband and our past. I knew this was a pivotal moment in the release of my past. It was long overdue. All things related to my ex stayed there that day. If I never do another healing, it was worth it just to leave him behind. I have not opened my medicine bag since that day, and I have had no desire to do any other work with it.

That day, I would pay attention to the approach of how to work with spirit and the ancestors of the Hawaiian lands. It wasn't much different from how I had been trained in my Peruvian shaman traditions. I took notice of the ceremony rhythm (beginning, middle, end) by setting an intention for the outcome, performing the ceremony, then thanking all the helping spirits for being present and letting them know the work was done. I realized that I had forgotten about these stages when doing my ego-center garage healing for Shiitake, but I also realized it was a great way to approach all aspects of life, not just an occasional healing session. I had once learned this same approach in a sales job I had; I must set my intention for the sales call, perform it, then follow up with thank you notes or proposals. All lessons learned in my spiritual practices always had many ways of applying to "real life" situations. I found, eventually, there is no separation. But there are things that numb us from connecting with spirit or cause us to forget basic "graces." By finding ways to relate to spirit, one can begin to find ways of relating to self or others. I will begin to walk you through the ways I have found that have shifted me from a place of being "the wounded" to a place of being "the experienced." As I shifted out of my wounded self, a whole new world opened up for me. My goal is to open up a whole new world for you by the time you finish this book. I think you will see that it's possible to shift your thinking to shift your life.

Tips for Flowing with Spirit:

- We all have to start somewhere, but step away from instructions and specific methods, take the training wheels off, and flow with spirit. Find tools and ways to relate to self and spirit that work best for you. We limit our power by trying to conform. Free yourself.

- Learn to follow the beat of your own drum and be cautious of conformity and entrancing and mind-numbing materialism. Create and follow your own dreams. Don't try to fit in or keep up with social media, TV, and other media's expectations of who you should be or what you should be doing. The ego and social conditioning can guide our thoughts and beliefs outside of ourselves and cause us to feel empty, lost, or depressed. But our soul's true nature is to connect with spirit, source, or God, and to live a meaningful life.

- Choose the road of spirit versus the road of ego and life will get easier for you. Surrender to spirit and be guided.

- The outer world is a reflection of our inner state of consciousness. Adjust accordingly.

- Lose "the story" and run with spirit. All the "but my family," "but my friends," and other excuses don't work in the spirit world. Wounds are simply experiences. Be thankful for them and move on. They are there for reference if needed, but don't become them.

Connecting with the Aina, Kupua, and Huna

A kind of peace began to settle over me following these events. My past was in the past, and my present and future thoughts seemed to become my awareness. I wasn't as restless living on an island in the middle of the ocean. I had struggled with it on and off after Shiitake died; it had been hard to move on, but I knew if I trusted in God's choice to take her back home, lived with the idea that she wasn't meant to stay, and honored her trip home, I could live at first for her and then for me. When the energy of my ex left, I was able to see the blessing of sharing in the initial excitement of Maui with Shiitake (and Patrick). Instead of feeling sad when I went to places Shiitake had gone with me, I smiled and knew she would always be there with me in spirit. My ex wasn't!

A certain excitement happens upon first arriving on Maui. Many people have experienced it. You feel that you must visit and see everything immediately, and you can't believe you live there. After a bit of time, however, some people go through an island fever experience when they realize how far away their loved ones are. Then you take a few trips back to the mainland, and after some more time, you begin to realize how fast-paced the rest of the world is. You see how modernized and materialistic many people on the mainland are and how they are disconnected with the land, which you learn to respect in Hawaii. The land (the a'ina) and nature have long been healing forces in my life, and they are so important in Hawaiian culture.

On Maui, you rise with the sun and you sleep when it sets. You begin to watch the butterflies, hear the birds, and look out upon the valleys to determine where the weather is good and where it is bad. Maui is made up of what we call micro-climates. Each area has its own vibe and weather. It's like you get to experience every climate in all parts of the world in one day when you leave your home. You begin to see the cycles of the day, the weather, the tourists, the locals, and you see a giant system—a flowing mass of life. It is much more apparent here than any place I've ever lived or visited. When you see the cycle of planes coming and going and cruise ships docking weekly, you see that you are lucky to be here.

But there is a side to Maui many don't see. It can be a very expensive place to live (or visit) and the cost of living is high. Many come here with a dream but are forced to go back home to survive or stay and become homeless. A huge drug problem exists here, too. And when people become homeless here, there is no way they can afford a plane ticket to leave, plus government assistance and housing is limited. I have now helped more homeless people with extra income, food, clothing, and other supplies than I have in any other place I have lived. An aloha spirit comes over you here where you begin to feel your neighbor's pain. When someone is hurt or goes without it is not simply someone else's issue. Everyone becomes family. And in this mass of humanity, you begin to see many reflections of self. A certain energy comes over you once you move here; some people say Mother Maui will have her way with you. I think it's like a college hazing experience, really. If she doesn't scare you away, and you stay, then she relaxes you, cares for you, loves you deeply, and makes you more carefree about self—but not careless.

Many come to Hawaii to heal. Hawaii is believed by many to be part of or near the lost continent of "Mu" or Lemuria. Many people who have experienced healing life changes in Hawaii have also claimed to have had recurring dreams and memories in early childhood of Ancient Lemuria. The islands are said to have many ancient vortexes that are now being triggered to open in our time. And the Maya, Inca, Tibetan, Hindu, and Aztec civilizations are said to have their origins in Lemuria.

Now that I was in Hawaii, I was starting to understand what the shaman in Peru had meant when he told me I would become a great shaman. I was meant to experience shamanic healing from a new perspective and it seemed to be coming full circle back to its roots.

In Hawaiian, the term for shaman is *kupua*, and it means a healer of relationships between mind and body, between people, between people and circumstances, between humans and nature, and between matter and spirit. Hawaiian Shamanism is said to follow "the way of the adventurer," as opposed to "the way of the warrior," which most people follow in other shamanic traditions. The adventurer is said to teach you how to harmonize your energy so you remain calm and even become a source of healing for another.

It is said, in most shamanic traditions, that the spirits will choose the person to be initiated as a shaman and that it is not necessarily a personal choice but a part of one's destiny. The word shaman comes from the Tungus tribe in Siberia and means "spiritual healer" or "one who sees in the dark." In a nutshell, a shaman interacts with the helping spirits to remedy the spiritual aspects of an illness; he travels into hidden realms to shift emotional and physical aspects of his client or community and heal them.

The Hawaiian shaman (or kupua) primarily work with the mind and body alone. Unlike other traditions, they don't use dreams to induce altered states, nor masks to assume other forms or qualities. The nature of shamanism is such that when you are healing others you are healing yourself, and while you are transforming the planet, you are transforming yourself. But what is fascinating is that it's almost engrained in the culture. Few would actually call themselves shaman, but many simply have been shown the ways and live without special acknowledgment or a title. It's the magic really of the Hawaiian islands, and it's a true blessing to live in this land and among its people.

Hawaiian shamanism begins with the myth of Maui, who is said to be a magician, trickster, demigod, miracle worker, luck bringer, and the most renowned spirit in Polynesian myth. (Not-so-jokingly, I think I've already met him!) The female being of Polynesian lore was Hina, goddess of the moon and mother of Maui. They call her "Mother Maui."

Many centuries ago, Hawaiian spiritual masters concluded that an aspect of consciousness operates covertly and indirectly (the subconscious) and another aspect of consciousness functions openly and directly (the conscious mind); finally, a super-consciousness encompasses both. These three consciousnesses form the whole of the human being. I was a bit shocked to find the alteration of the mind was so much at the heart of Hawaiian ways because it's all so much more than just a vacation destination with surf and sun.

Max Freedom Long, an American author who lived in Hawaii, wrote extensively about Hawaiian spiritual practices. "Huna" is a word he adopted to describe his theory of metaphysics and the spiritual practices of the ancient Hawaiian kahunas. He believed the secrets of the Hawaiian spiritual beliefs were encoded in the language itself and he attempted to chronicle those beliefs. Long believed he had discovered an ancient Truth, not just about Hawaiian spirituality but one that linked back to India and ancient Egypt. He believed Hawaiians were a lost tribe of Berbers. He wrote that spiritual masters migrated to Hawai'i from Egypt, passing on to the priests of India some of their basic beliefs. He examined parallels between his invented system of Huna and religions such as Hinduism, Buddhism, and Christianity. He also linked Huna to Theosophy and New Thought movements and he believed Christian Scientists understood positive thinking better than any group he knew. He encouraged his readers to subscribe to Unity Church beliefs. Later, Huna teachers have firmly placed his beliefs within the New Age movement, claiming that Huna originally came from the aliens from the Pleiades, who were remnants of the mythical advanced civilizations of Mu or Lemuria, and the aliens associated the islands with chakras, vortexes (condensed energy sources), and lay lines (alignments to numerous places of geological and historical interest, such as ancient monuments).

On a side note: the Hawaiian word for "volcano" also means "pyramid." Mauna Loa and Kilauea volcanoes on the Big Island are actually said to be the biggest pyramids of all. Hawaii (Maui in particular) has been referred to by many as the heart chakra, or heart center, for the planet.

"The intuitive mind is a sacred gift and
the rational mind is a faithful servant.
We have created a society that honors the servant
and has forgotten the gift."

— Albert Einstein

Huna starts with the belief that three levels of self exist:

Three Levels of Self:

Ku: The heart, body, or subconscious. The Ku is that aspect of consciousness that contains our memories, helps us learn, remember, develop skills, and maintain the body's balance.

The essential aspect of memory is that it is stored in the body as a vibration or movement pattern. Releasing the memories will generally lead to a healing.

Lono: The mind or conscious mind. The mind aspect, Lono, is that part of you that is consciously aware of internal and external input. It includes all sensations, memories, thoughts, movement, and time. The *Lono* directs what we are focused on, which directs our attention and decisions. Intent is a kind of decision making that directs awareness as well as activity. You have the power to manage your *Ku*, through the *Lono*, which will bring tremendous effects on health, happiness, and success—either positively or negatively…it is up to you! Lastly, the primary tool of the *Lono* is imagination, the development of which is paramount to the shaman. For with the intended use of your imagination, you can influence and direct your aspects and the world you are part of.

Kane: The spirit or superconscious. The spirit aspect is also the source aspect of spiritual energy. Its primary function is creativity in the form of mental and physical expression. To explore your spiritual connection, sit comfortably and close your eyes. Take a few deep breaths, and be aware of your body. Now imagine and focus on your breath intensely. In a moment or so, you may feel sensations of relaxation, pleasure, or energy. Then you will have made a conscious contact with your *Kane*. At this point, you may engage in a communication process with the experience. One of the best ways for communicating directly with your *Kane* is to say, “Thank you.” Thank you for the good things that are and for the good

> that is coming. Finish the exercise with a positive phrase that signifies to you a completion. I suggest: "So be it."

The Seven Principles of Huna are not a part of traditional Hawaiian beliefs and they are influenced by West-African shamanism. Huna was developed by Serge Kahili King, Ph.D. Although Huna does deviate some from authentic Hawaiian tradition, Huna teachers provide excellent healing. Huna is said to mean "secret." Huna is believed to have the ability to influence consciousness. It's not restricted to human consciousness, but may include the consciousnesses of animals, rocks, and everything in the world around us, seen and unseen. Therefore, it can include gods, goddesses, and the spirits of the departed, who often appear in the form of animals. These principles are said to govern life and the creation of all existence. These might be considered "healing practices for the mind and body" and they are at the core of Hawaiian lomilomi massage as well. The seven fundamental principles are:

The First Principle: IKE—The World Is What You Think It Is (pronounced E'-kay)

> Life is a matter of point of view. Whatever you believe, you will manifest. Truth is what you define as such. Thoughts of fear, worry, anger, and resentment can make us sick and diminish our effectiveness, while thoughts of confidence, determination, love, and forgiveness can make us well and increase our performance. The metaphysical realm gives us the idea that thoughts will attract their equivalent. This is the Law of Attraction: like attracts like. Positive thoughts will attract positive people and events; negative thoughts will attract negative

people and events. The first principle of this philosophy is the power of thought in the form of prayer, faith, and conviction to change physical conditions, events, and circumstances. Everything we experience is interpreted according to our own beliefs and reality. There is no universal reality for all people. Your brain is creating the world you see, just like it is creating the world you experience every time you have a vivid dream at night. The Huna shamans believe our life is another form of a dream. They also believe we dream on different levels and have several layers of dreams. The only difference for us between a dream and "reality" is whether others have the same experience. In other words, it is basically our own dream. We can wake up from the dream (or life) and build a new dream (or life).

The ancient Hawaiians believed in four levels of reality. The kupua (Hawaiian priest, shaman, or sorcerer) learned to move between these realities to gain a greater understanding for himself and those he was aiding. The four levels of reality are:

Ike Papakahi: Objective (facts, scientific reality). Our conscious and physical state of the body. Objective reason.

Ike Papalua: Subjective (psychic reality). Intuition, psychic or telepathic experiences, and all other input outside of the objective facts are taken into account. We are not separate from anything, and a connection exists between you and the things you feel connected with.

Ike Papakolu: Symbolic (shamanic reality). All of our experience is seen as a dream. Everything is dreaming its own dream. We interpret everything going on around us as symbolic in nature. There is no "coincidence" in this level of reality. Everything is a symbol for something.

Ike Papaha: Wholistic (mystical reality). The reality is that everything in the universe is "one." You are interconnected with everything, so you take care of everything, not just yourself.

The Second Principle: KALA—There Are No Limits; Everything is Possible

The universe is infinite. There are no limits to your life other than those you define yourself. Kala teaches that we are all interconnected; your actions and thoughts influence the universe, and the universe influences you. When you allow yourself to expand and open your mind, you will naturally seek out new pathways and, ultimately, change what is possible. There are two kinds of limitations, creative and filtered:

Creative Limitation: assumes the purposeful establishment of limits within an infinite universe in order to create particular experiences. Our realm of physical experience is limited by our senses (the frequencies of sight, sound, touch, gravity, distance, and time). A shaman does not deny the existence or usefulness of rules and limits, but uses them to reach his goals.

Filtered Limitation: is imposed by ideas and beliefs that inhibit creativity rather than enhance it. They generate focus without the potential for positive action—hopelessness for example. Emotions, in general, are these limits. You can limit joy.

The Third Principle: MAKIA—Energy Flows Where Attention Goes (pronounced Mu-kee-a

Whatever you spend most of your time thinking about will grow into your reality. Create focused goals and direction. This concept can be compared to the difference between a lightbulb and a laser beam. If you are fuzzy about anything, you will draw more fuzziness into your life, but with laser clear and precise focus it's like having your eye on the prize. Makia is used by many shaman and yogis. Meditation and hypnosis are examples of makia. Meditation itself simply means to think deeply and continuously. You are meditating whenever you are engaged in sustained focused attention on anything. Meditation is considered to be more spiritual, and is used for cleaning karma and reaching enlightenment. Hypnosis is a condition of sustained attention, just like meditation. Energy flows where attention goes. What is part of your present life experience is a result of habitual, sustained, and focused attention and awareness. If you don't like what you see, then you need to find some way to shift your attention into a new pattern.

The Fourth Principle: Manawa—Now Is the Moment of Power (pronounced Ma-nah-wa)

In the Hawaiian tradition, the past did not give you what you have today, nor make you what you are today. *It is your be-*

liefs, decisions, and actions today about yourself and the world around you that give you what you have and make you what you are. Karma exists and operates only in the present moment. Your environment and circumstances in this moment are the direct reflections of your mental and physical behavior in this moment. This moment is where you can facilitate change. This moment is where you connect with, support, and allow healing for yourself and others. This moment. Thanks to memory, we may carry over habits from day to day, but each day is a new creation, and any habit can be changed in any present moment. Genes are not necessarily an influencing factor, but your beliefs about them are. Today's actions create tomorrow's successes. No action today creates no action tomorrow. Ask yourself: What small action can I do now to bring me closer to my vision?

The Fifth Principle: ALOHA—To Love Is to Be Happy With

In Hawaiian, a*loha* is the word for love. Alo means "to be with, to share an experience, here and now." *Oha* means "affection, joy." Aloha means many things, but it can be loosely translated as "*to love is to be happy with.*" This means that love exists to the degree that you are happy with the object of your love.

In any relationship—whether with a person, place, or thing—the happy part comes from love and the unhappy part comes from fear, anger, and doubt. To be deeply in love means to be deeply connected. Fear, anger, and doubt are removed as the depth and clarity of the connection increases.

The Sixth Principle: MANA—All Power Comes from Within

Hawaiian philosophy teaches that all the power that creates your experience comes from your own body, mind, and spirit. Mana recognizes that we all come from the same place—spirit. There are no limits; the Universe or Source of Life is infinite, and because it is infinite, all of its power is at every point of it, including the point you define as you. Basically, nothing ever happens to you without your participation. Every event you experience you creatively attract through your beliefs, desires, fears, and expectations. You either react to it habitually or you begin to understand you can make yourself unhappy. Others won't act the way you want them to or the way you think they should. It is important to change the factors in yourself. Because the power was in you to create it, the power is also in you to change it. You must define your own experience. Others have no power over you unless you give it to them. Defining yourself as a victim gives away your power. Try stating this each day to yourself: "Today, I am creating my life with the next decision I make."

The Seventh Principle: PONO—Effectiveness Is the Measure of Truth

This principle teaches that you are most effective when you are in alignment with your truth. The means determines the end. Violent means will produce violent results; peaceful means will produce peaceful results. Reaching success through ruthlessness will produce a state of success in which others will act ruthlessly toward you; reaching success through helping others will produce a state of success in which others are helping

> you. This principle also says: What is really important is what works. If it brings you contentment and joy, it is a good measurement that you are on the right path. Pono also means doing what is right, ethical, moral, correct, and finding alignment or "right-ness." If what you are doing is effective, then you are pono with it. I have a sticker on the back of my car that says "*pono means do what's right.*"

It has been said that each of these principles inter-relates with the other principles, and like our world, they are all interconnected. As you work with them, they will teach and inform your life, your practice, and all of your relationships. If we were to adopt these methods in our daily lives and not just use them for healing when we identify a problem, then we'd likely all become our own healers. If we would adopt any of these methods to help us awaken and transform, the world would be a better place. Our children would be taught morals and beliefs that would showcase the fact that we are not here alone and left to figure life out by ourselves; rather, we are here to support and love all sentient beings and make the world a better place—whether that is in our personal/spiritual lives or our business lives.

IKE PRINCIPLE EXERCISE:

To better understand your beliefs about yourself and how you relate to this principle, *quickly* fill in the blanks. Go off the top of your head. The answers you come up with are where your true thoughts and intentions are right now so it's best to not spend too much time thinking about it.

- I think people are...

- I think I am…
- I think my health is…
- I think the world is…
- I think my financial power is…
- I think my ability to experience love, joy, ecstasy is…
- I think my job is…
- I limit my thoughts by…
- I limit my reality by…
- My negative attention is on…
- My positive attention is on…
- My thoughts at this moment are…
- I love…
- My fears are…
- My desires are…
- I am an expert in…
- I think… < you may come up with anything else that is in your life here >

This is your current truth. Now you might see why your reality is the way it is. This is what the world is reflecting back to you. Do you like it? Do you want to change it?

Now, walk back through the IKE principles again with a more positive outlook and see whether you can create a list of positive affirmations or thoughts you can live by. If you change your belief patterns, your world will change. For example, you might say, "I think the world is sad, depressing, and unfair." Remember, the world is what you think it is. Do you realize that you might just be creating a world that is sad, depressing, and unfair with your subconscious beliefs? Give it a try.

How could you shift your feelings and beliefs to live a more positive and fruitful life?

If you follow the shaman's thought process that everything is a dream, then you might begin to realize that every answer you come up with is for you, and it's based on personal choice. Truth is what you define as such. How well is this working for you? What limits have you set for yourself?

Ho'oponopono

Ho'oponopono is believed to be an ancient Hawaiian healing practice of forgiveness and reconciliation. Some disagree with whether to call it true to Hawaiian ways, and they suggest that if we are in need of forgiving ourselves and others, then we are not living by the right standards. I tend to agree. Nonetheless, it has shown some effectiveness in healing so I have included it here. It is used as a practice of healing after breaking spiritual laws, for a mental cleansing, to restore relationships, and as a process to get to the state of zero where we would have no memories or identity. The word "Ho'oponopono" means "to make right"—to make right with your relationships and with all others; to make right if you have done harm, whether intentionally or accidentally; to make right for any mistakes you have made; and to make right for the mistakes and errors of others as well.

The modern day Hawaiian psychologist, Dr. Ihaleakala Hew Len, worked in a prison for the criminally insane. Len made history by healing and releasing a whole ward of inmates by using the ancient Hawaiian healing technique of Ho'oponopono. Len also co-authored a book with Joe Vitale called *Zero Limits.* His method was also practiced by the late Japanese healer Masaru Emoto to heal water. I had the honor of doing a ceremony with Masaru Emote while on one of my visits to Peru in 2009. Both of these men practiced a simple prayer or mantra where the individual recites (and wholeheartedly means) the following as a process for healing:

"I love you.
I am sorry.
Please forgive me.
Thank you."

The prayer is based on Len's idea of 100 percent responsibility—taking responsibility for everyone's actions, not only for our own. Everything we see, hear, taste, touch, or in any way experience is our responsibility because it is in our life. The problem is not with our external reality; it is with ourselves. To change our reality, we have to change ourselves. Everything exists as a projection from inside the human being, and all consciousness is part of the whole. Any error a person clears in his or her own consciousness should be cleared for everyone. Citing the prayer—spoken without meaning and emotion—would not be as powerful without also understanding the concepts behind it.

Len was a student of a female healing kahuna named Morrnah Simeona, who had slightly different beliefs. Simeona describes problems only as the effects of negative karma, saying, "You have to experience by yourself what you have done to others." The belief that we create our life circumstances was common knowledge to ancient peoples, as was the idea of "things we had brought with us from other lifetimes." She did not use mantras or other exercises. Len believed the main objective of Ho'oponopono is to wipe your slate clean and get back to your "zero state." This is said to be a pure clean slate we were born with before our memories and identity were created in this lifetime. Again, I argue, if you have done nothing wrong then what needs to be forgiven?

Much of the healing practice of the Ho'oponopono way encourages us to rely more on what our instincts (and our senses) tell us so that we can better appreciate life. Nature is also believed to help us make our decisions. The interesting thing about Ho'oponopono is that when you are working on healing yourself, you are actually healing others. (Many other healing practices talk about how when you work on others you are healing yourself.) It is the idea of taking complete responsibility for whatever shows up in your life...including others' actions, and not just your own. It implies that *to change your reality, you need to change yourself.* As you change your inner self, you change the world outside of yourself as well. Maybe you've heard the saying, "Heal yourself and you heal the world."

The historical Ho'oponopono process begins with prayer, a statement of the problem, and then a discussion. Family members are expected to work out problems and cooperate. Everyone's feelings are acknowledged. One or more periods of silence may be taken for reflection. Then confession, repentance, and forgiveness take place. Everyone releases (*kala*) each other, letting go. They cut off the past (*'oki*), and together they close the event with a ceremonial feast, called *pani*, which often includes eating seaweed, symbolic of the release. Giving the person forgiven a lei made from the fruit of the hala tree is another tradition.

From Wounded to Aware

I knew of these healers and techniques before I moved to Maui because the concepts were briefly discussed in my shaman healing classes. But, fascinatingly, upon my arrival, the land, people, and culture began to teach me these lessons inherently. Shiitake's sickness and Bella's rescue would enhance my learning. I wasn't even aware I was learning or healing. The island has a way with you, and all learned techniques seem to go by the wayside as you develop a kind of claircognizance (a knowing) for the Hawaiian ways. It's almost an absorption process, as if you are a sponge. I've often told Patrick there is a kind of innocence on Maui, like being in the Garden of Eden. But Maui will have its way with you if you are not listening. The land was awakening me. As traumatic events were happening, I was learning, and in the calm or down times, I was trying to understand how to take what I had learned in both my yoga and Peruvian-based shamanic training and apply it to each life scenario.

I found that the Ho'oponopono was a great tool for the psychology of the mind, and the huna principles gave me something that my Peruvian-based shamanic training didn't. I had been shown how to heal myself and others in the Peruvian tradition, but I hadn't been shown how to live life better so that I would no longer need the healing. The huna principles would assist me in moving into a different level of understanding, but I think it was only possible for me to utilize them after a certain level of healing had already occurred. I wouldn't have been ready to understand or learn them prior to a basic level of healing. I suspect if they were principles I was raised with, I wouldn't have needed to begin with the elementary healing. I believe the awakening needed to occur before the transformation could begin. I thought I had spent many years awakening, but now I believe it comes in cycles—and as we spin through one evolutionary cycle completely, we begin another. We awaken, transform, realize, and then stand in a place of being with that self until we go through it all once again. It's like peeling the endless layers of an onion. In each revolution we are more awakened and aware than the last.

Tips for Stepping Into Your Becoming:

1. It's easier to heal yourself and others when you step out of your ego.
2. Find a tool that works for you to clear your mind.
3. Find a system of beliefs or principles to adopt and live by them.

EXERCISE:

How have these Hawaiian principles played out in your life? _______

____
____
____
____
____
____
____
____
____
____
____
____

How could these Hawaiian principles play out in your life? ________

Walk back through the Huna principles with whatever issue is most present in your mind. Did they help you find a solution or give you action items to follow up on? Define your action plan below.

PART 2

TRANSFORM

Spiritual transformation can sometimes feel like you are losing control of your life and you are left questioning your identity. But when you go through the "dark night of the soul" it can also be an indication of strength and spiritual and emotional maturity. The Bible calls this shift a journey through the "valley of the shadow of death." In ancient Egypt, India, and Greece, schools of wisdom developed to help people though the process. Many times, people were taken into seclusion and taught "inner mysteries" or spiritual truths. Transformation can help us to become a conscious creator in accordance with divine will. But in our Western world, little support exists for people undergoing a spiritual transformation. Regardless, this transformation begins with the self. To succeed in this process, one must surrender the ego and develop a certain level of trust in the divine. Many today believe we humans are leaving the Picean age and entering the Aquarian age; the earth is a living being who is transforming herself, thus transforming all those living on her. In a nutshell, the Aquarian age is about enlightenment. The earth is also moving into a higher vibration. All who live on her will go through some kind of spiritual transformation, and she will showcase her changes with natural shifts like climate change.

Your spiritual transformation may have you questioning yourself, your interpretation of life, your purpose, your concerns, and the deepest aspects of the human spirit. Your transformation may be self-induced or come

about through a divine act. In either case, you were meant to live a simpler, freer, more loving life. Shifting deeply through what hasn't worked is sometimes the only way to get you to what will. The comparison can be useful for becoming consciously aware of your growth and beginning to step into new possibilities. I often asked myself what the purpose of transforming all aspects of my life was as I was going through it, but then I realized it was about transformation from who I am into who I am meant to become. Who are you meant to become?

"Everybody comes to a point in their life when they want to quit. But it's what you do at that moment that determines who you are."

— David Goggins

AWAKEN — TRANSFORM — REALIZE

Chapter 4

Stepping Into Your Healed Self

"Man suffers only because he takes seriously what the gods made for fun."

— Alan W. Watts

To heal, it's critical to make internal changes. I have spent many years being unhappy, but not much can be accomplished from a place of sadness, angst, sorrow, and depression. Our current human experience does indeed take its toll on us. Living the lifestyles we live, it can be difficult to maintain a positive state of mind, especially when we see so many things on our planet that need to change. But it's not easy to change what we would like to unless we do it from a positive, peaceful state. Happiness is no doubt an inside job that we choose to bring into our lives—it's a choice! And we can change the way we feel just by changing our thoughts. Ultimately, though, all experiences serve as opportunities for growth. Positive emotions—feelings of love, gratitude, compassion, and many more—have a powerful effect on us and others because our consciousness plays a big role in the creation of our reality. *Perhaps by coming into the physical, we are meant to have challenges, just to tempt the sacredness of our response?* It's much harder to hold a positive and faithful opinion about something when it feels the world is falling apart around you.

Yogi Bhajan talked about how the Aquarian age (the time we are living in now) is a special time in the evolution of human consciousness; he said people's sensitivity is changing and the pressure of the world is provoking us to become "self-sensory humans." He said:

> "Self-sensory humans will be deeply sincere, and will perceive and act on the fact that they are factual—a fact of life; a fact of existence born in the image of God. The time of self-value has come and it is time "to be, to BE," to know that "I am, I AM." It is *not a time to search for God* but to *be God*; not to trust in God, but to *dwell in the workings of God."*

Yogi Bhajan pushed his students to stop searching and begin practicing, to accept and help each other as equals. He suggested that our presence is our purity. He said our nobility is projection. He taught that life was not given to us so we could play or so we could experience traumas. Life was given to us to *experience life.* Life is about caliber (the quality of our character), and it's given to us once, so it's not meant to be wasted in games. He believed we have two options: to serve the ego, or to serve the truth. He said there are three ways to live: *live by your spirit, live by your mind*, or *live by your ego.* He believed you can't live by the mind because it is etheric (and goes back and forth), so you have to live by your spirit or your ego. If you live by the ego, you try to live the way you want, not the way the universe wants. He thought we should live to be what we should be, not what we are and that we should die being grateful being for who we are. He believed we could do anything if we have caliber and intuition because that gives you grit and stamina. He also said if you are kind to others God will be kind to you. He believed that every relationship is based on each person's level of emotional security.

He said that the mind needs to have a base of character with commitment. All facets of the human body have to be controlled and characterized by this character of commitment, and they have to be tested by the principal of commitment. He said that what makes you great is when you project to make the impossible possible. You, reality, and God are a unity, a non-dual presence in every moment. The exploration of your character begins with the do's and don'ts, and the discovery of your depth and virtues happens with challenges and tests. Character is a property of consciousness, and each person must live true to his or her infinite self for harmony to exist.

So, the question might become: "How do I live true to the infinite self?" Do we walk around believing we are gods? Well, in a sense, yes! The way I sometimes look at this is that I imagine: What if there were no God? No heaven? No "happy place" we go to or connect to? No big ship that picks us up when we are tired of being here? I've gone deep down the road into many years of depression and waited for someone or something to rescue me, but guess what? I'm still here! No one comes to get you but *you*! And when Bella was on that cliff, I was forced to let go of my ego because the situation was not about what I wanted, but what the universe wanted, what Bella needed for her growth, and what I needed for my growth. It's always sounded a bit fruity or vague to me to have this kind of "wait for God" approach because I thought if I sat back, I was lazy. There is a fine line. Wouldn't it be much easier to wait for things to come with the grace of God than breaking your back, your heart, and your spirit in trying to find them? But isn't the search part of the journey? There is a fine line. But how is that happy place found? If I don't try, will I get to live my ultimate life? Character is built by the tests life brings, and those "tests" might actually be pre-planned to a degree.

If, as I believe, my soul did decide to incarnate into the physical, then I imagine I would have set a plan in motion somewhere along the way to suggest the "tests" that might best aid it in its growth. If I wanted to understand heartache, perhaps I would set up a "test" to break my heart and a path for successfully maneuvering my way through it. And to master heartache, I might choose it again and again until I learned from it. But the question remains: Why would I do that? We have a purpose when we incarnate into the physical; perhaps that purpose is because our souls cannot feel as deeply when we are not in carbon life form. Perhaps it is not as easy to understand love if we don't understand heartache and loss. But if we believe we need loss to understand love, then wouldn't we just get more loss? If energy flows where energy goes, then perhaps we should let God show us the most graceful time on our journey into love and forget about the concept of loss. And perhaps that means when we are happy with life, we are shown more love…provided all power, decision, and outcome ultimately comes from a decision within. What is your choice? To dwell on loss or to dwell in love? Or perhaps I should ask you: What do you want to attract more of?

"You are an aperture through which the universe is looking at and exploring itself."

— Alan W. Watts

What Is Your Reflection?

As if you have entered a world of mirrors, all that you encounter in life becomes a reflection of you. At various stages in my life, I stepped out of the chaos of life to ask myself where the reflection of me resided within the scenario. It's a practice I've developed for myself over the course of much time on my healing path. It's easy to find what you need to heal when stopping to reflect on what (and who) is around you. Take a moment to look around. What do you see in others that bothers you the most? Where is that within you? What do you like the most in others around you, and how is that also in you? And then take inventory of where you live and what you like and dislike. How do you create your environment? What is there that you wish to change? Do you live in chaos but want peace? Is your home cluttered and messy and you want simple and easy? How do your thoughts influence your surroundings?

I recently met a woman who was helping a homeless family. Other things going on in her life didn't present themselves as apparently to me as her relationship with this homeless family. I knew to pay attention to the piece that came to me. I knew I could donate a few small things and a bit of cash, and I could ask others around me to help. Others around me donated simply by me asking. Not only did the reality of the homeless family fill my awareness, but so did all things related to belongings and worthiness. This family was perceived to have less than each of us who donated. We all felt sorry for them. But I knew they were there to show me I had taken things for granted in my own life. I wanted to own a home, but I didn't; however, they couldn't even afford to rent one. I wanted more, but they had so much less. I wanted a house with a garage to park my car in, but there they were living on the beach in a tent and sharing one car. At one point, I became aware that the mother stayed home to guard her family's possessions while the husband worked; then I began to ask myself why I was aware of this; how did it reflect me and what was I to learn from it? Was she not feeling worthy enough to seek and have employment? Was she just more comfortable with her belongings? How did that represent me?

Having left my career behind me so many years earlier, did I also not know that I had the power to be my own human, my own boss, and an income generator? I forgot that I once didn't think twice about any of this. I just went out and did it. But the reflection of her showed me that I was stronger than I gave myself credit for. I forgot that I used to be much more powerful in my career and money-making potential. But when you go through so much change, transformation, and pain, you can feel defeated. Even though I once made an independent, six-figure income, I had forgotten that I once had done that and was unaware that I could do it again. I felt small in myself and my achievements because life had become so hard for a few years. I forgot my power. This homeless mother and wife may not have ever known a six-figure income, but this was how her story presented itself to me. The reflection I saw meant I needed to change my thinking and re-find my strength. Where did that powerful corporate executive in me go? And, even more, did I want her back?

At the time when this homeless family came into my awareness, Patrick and I were looking to buy our first home on Maui. Patrick had gone through a divorce five years earlier and had a few financial challenges that got under my skin, but the reflection of me in that situation was that I felt he was the one who needed to get the house because I didn't believe I had the power to do so. But, as we looked at homes, I found another mirror within myself. A home we liked was in the middle of a divorce settlement, and we wanted to make an offer on it. We eventually did, but due to the owners' divorce, the negotiating went back and forth, which became very challenging. Again, this was a great mirror not for just me, but for Patrick as well. I saw the pain of the woman and knew she wanted to stay on Maui, but the husband took a job in New Mexico. I'm guessing this may have caused some friction in the marriage as well. I was feeling her pain, but others were judging her as not being competent. I saw that selling the house for her represented the idea that she was moving on. The house on Maui was beautiful, so I'm sure it was a dream fulfilled for them at one point in their lives. And I'm sure there was a battle waging between them over all things financial as well. So I saw the pain in her and it reminded me of my own divorce. It stirred up old wounds. I realized I still had more to heal within myself, so I should not have become frustrated with her. Instead I became thankful. The offer we submitted was rejected and much time passed going back and forth just to get a response from this couple. I'm sure they had communication issues going on, and being in different time zones and states didn't help. While all this back and forth was going on, it was weighing heavily on my mind. What was I meant to heal? Why was this so difficult? How could I help? Where was my reflection? I was a student of the reflection, and I began watching it closely because its presence was really a gift to help me heal. Where has a reflection like this come into your awareness? Did you notice it and take action to heal it? How did you do that? Perhaps awareness is the simple tool for healing it.

"Letting go gives us freedom,
and freedom is the only condition for happiness.

If, in our heart, we still cling to anything anger, anxiety, or possessions we cannot be free."

— Thích Nhat Hanh

Walking Your Story Through the Chakras

I jumped into the shower one morning with the house and this couple heavily on my mind. I started to talk to the woman's subconscious as if I were talking to her in the flesh. I began by telling her I was sorry, and I had deep love for her. I thought about the ways of Ho'oponopono, so I also asked for her forgiveness because we were "taking" this home from her. I explained that we were hopeful to put our divorces behind us, and this was a new chance for us. I was hopeful she would see and understand this, but I wasn't sure whether any of it would become a part of her awareness. I then recalled that Ho'oponopono is not about me healing her but about me healing me, so I looked at myself and at every aspect of her and her situation that was mirrored within me. I started to cry as the water from the shower ran down my back and over my tears.

In my past healing work, I knew that looking into these issues might be best done while visiting each chakra. I knew that wounds settle there in the energy centers. Despite everything I had just learned of the Hawaiian ways, I still fell back upon my old healing ways to cleanse her energetic system as well as my own. I had been taught a technique for cleaning out the chakras in my shamanic training classes, but this self-taught technique I was about to use would require me to look at each chakra individually with our common stories in mind.

After looking at the story as a whole, I started at the base of the spine between the legs at the first chakra, which represents stability, groundedness, and all things home. I took my fingers and motioned the energy backwards and counter-clockwise to clean it out. When the chakras are spinning correctly, they go clockwise. A pendulum can be used to determine the direction, but after so many years of doing it, the process just comes naturally to me now. I don't have to think about it since it's just like brushing my teeth. So I spun it backwards and imagined pulling out all kinds of gunk and letting it wash down the drain in the hot shower water. I saw that she and I and even the homeless woman all needed to be better grounded and comforted in all things related to home, marriage, and relationship with self. We were all tied together. When I was healing myself, I was praying for their healing, too. By seeing your self in others, you can help heal those you interact with as well.

I saw that when a person is not grounded, nothing else works or flows in her life. If I feel the need to protect my things or fight against someone else for them, it causes disharmony within me. I cannot fully open my heart or feel in my power without being grounded. I finished up the cleaning of the first chakra and began to work my way up my spine. The second chakra would show me that creativity and healthy views and experiences on sexuality can only happen when a grounded sense of safety first exists. I was struggling with this myself, and I knew I couldn't be fully in our relationship until I could find a way to feel safe. I was unable to be as creative in all my endeavors unless I felt safe. In other words, I was blocked. The third chakra would teach me that to be empowered in myself, I first had to feel safe, and once I was safe, I could be creative and empowered.

It was all connecting like nothing else before. I had done this chakra healing countless times, but something about this shower healing session and the mirror of these woman was allowing me to heal so much more. Maybe I was just ready to be healed, too. I worked up to the forth chakra and felt my closed heart. I prayed that each woman would know what true love of self felt like. I knew I needed more self-love also. I knew that if I opened my heart more, I could open my voice more, as I moved to the fifth chakra at the throat. How can people represent themselves with voice if all other aspects of self are not balanced? I knew I needed to look at all of these issues within myself, but first I needed this mirror finally to see the "power of me." Who or what has given you this gift of reflection of self?

I began to cry in thankfulness to each woman for showing me myself and allowing me the opportunity to heal. I hoped that I had helped them in some small way. I felt them within me and as one. Each person comes into your life as an incredible opportunity to see your own reflection. I suddenly seemed to stop crying; then I felt very empowered and healed, as if none of my wounds had ever existed. I nearly leapt from the shower and ran downstairs to tell Patrick we were going to get that house because the woman was healed! But then I heard him on the phone with a client, and I also realized he just wouldn't understand what had happened in my empowering shower that day. My experience was only meant for me. Sometimes, profound experiences with self can't be explained and just really aren't meant to be shared. Whatever happened that day in the shower seemed to have better aligned me with my goals, because shortly thereafter, our offer was accepted—we were going to be buying our first house on Maui! Unfortunately, though, not before I fully let go of the wounds of my past. But fortunately, also with far more new memories to be made than old wounds to haunt.

Walking your story through the chakras for healing is a great way to gain a new understanding of how they reside in all your power centers and affect your life. Use this tool to help you find how each piece resides within you. I believe that through awareness, you can find healing and shift the energy and the mind. Walk it through the chakras:

EXERCISE:

Define your wound? ______________________________

____

____

____

____

____

____

How does your wound keep you from feeling safe? Grounded? __

____

____

____

____

____

____

____

____

____

Does it affect your creativity or sexuality? How? ________________

Describe how this wound takes your power away: ______________

Does your wound keep you from loving others? Yourself? Describe:

Does this wound rob you of your voice or affect how you tell your story or talk to others? Describe: ______________________

Use your intuition to define a solution. How can shifting the perspective you have change the outcome? Explain: ____________________

____

____

____

____

____

____

Not My Anniversary!

Around the same time, or just slightly prior to this event, I had a day that rather haunted me. I was telling my friend about how I rarely got sick now that I'd learned how to heal myself. I told her that when I feel an illness coming, I push it away energetically. Patrick has even commented that I'm never sick. He is also learning how to keep himself healthy as well, and he rarely "comes down" with something like he used to when we first met. I always believed all illness to be energetic, not something viral that you "catch." But just a half-hour after I told my friend "I never get sick," I suddenly had the most excruciating pain I have probably ever felt in my body. As I was drying off after coming out of the shower, I was in so much pain I started to drip sweat. I tried to get dressed, but I was so hot I took all my clothes off, and I looked as though I had just walked out of the shower, even though I had already toweled off. Not only was I sweating, but I couldn't stand up straight. I started to cry because not only did it hurt badly, but it scared the tar out of me. I was nervous and shaking and didn't know what to do. Patrick ran upstairs to kiss me goodbye and tell me, since it was Christmas break, he was off to the beach with his boys who were visiting from the mainland. He was excited to go and didn't notice my pain. That in itself brought more pain and more tears. How could he not notice my pain or acknowledge it the way I needed him to? I was in and out of consciousness and the room was spinning. Before I could even think, I suddenly flashed back to a previous lifetime. I was hardly conscious. It just happened so quickly.

There I was in another body, in another lifetime, lying in a bed, with a caretaker next to me. She was dark-skinned, African perhaps. She was wearing a dark blue dress with white ruffles on the edges and a matching blue nightcap; I think it was a nightgown from the late 1800s. I saw a man with Patrick's energy or soul, but his physical appearance was different from Patrick's current one. He was the one I saw in my visions of my past life. I had seen this lifetime once before. He was my husband and his two boys were my boys. I was dying in the bedroom in this vision/lifetime, and he was playing with the boys in the other room. They were running around, laughing and chasing each other. They were blonde boys. They were running around laughing.

I was flashing in and out of this other life. When I came back from the vision, I was lying sweating, in pain and naked, having removed my clothes to stay cool. Patrick was still there. I tried to tell him I needed to go to the hospital, but I could hardly speak. I was sure he hadn't heard me because he kissed me, said goodbye, and left. I couldn't react because I was hardly functioning. He had no idea what I was experiencing, and I was too weak to tell him. Before I knew it, he was gone. Then I came fully back into my body in my bed. I thought I'd have to drive myself to the hospital or call 911. But, thankfully, as dramatic as this seemed, there always seems to be some humor somewhere in my visions. I suddenly laughed and thought how funny I'd look driving to the hospital all sweaty and naked! I laughed and seemed to start feeling better almost immediately. This kind of thing has happened to me many times, but not accompanied with so much pain. And when this kind of thing happens now, I just seem to roll with it, shrug my shoulders, ask for some clarification, and move on. What else can you do?

I'm not sure what happened to transition me out of the vision, but maybe I just needed to see the correlation with the past life and the current one, or maybe I just needed to laugh. But I did suddenly see a message pop up on my phone from the same friend I had told I was never sick. I told her I'd never say that again, and then I told her what had happened. She asked where Patrick was and whether he was taking care of me. It didn't even dawn on me, but I wondered the same thing then. What happened to him, and why wasn't he here? All of a sudden, I felt very hurt and very alone. As I looked at the phone to respond, it all began to make some sense as I saw the date. It was my and my ex-husband's wedding anniversary. I realized that some kind of programming had gone off inside of me as a result. I was hurt that Patrick had left me. I was also hurt that my marriage had failed, that my ex had let me go, or that I had failed to be what he needed. I started to wonder whether my ex had even thought of me at all on this day. I was hurt that it was the day after Christmas and I was alone. I was hurt that I was in pain and disregarded.

A lot of healing had to take place here. I began to walk through each memory and each thought, and I told myself that this experience was not about blaming others. It was only about how I feel and how I heal this pain. This story involved other actors, so I could relate, but I knew if I could change my perception of the pain and hurt,

I could change the outcome. If I could change my expectations, I could change the outcome. No one knew how he or she had hurt me, but me. And I was the one who had allowed for the hurt to hurt so badly. It really had nothing to do with others and everything to do with me. This was my moment of power. My power needed to come from within. I was suffering, not them. I needed to let go of the illusion. The power to do so was in my mind.

I was also struggling with my age and the fact that I might likely never have kids in this lifetime. At forty-three, it was becoming a reality for me that it would never happen. Patrick was off with his kids, but mine just kept dying—I had lost my hairy children one after another. My dogs had become replacements for the children I would never have. The hardest part about having dogs as your children is they only live so long. In order to have one live as long as your child, or at least outlive me, it would need to live for fifty to sixty years. Instead, realistically five or six dogs would be needed to make up for the life of a child. This also meant five or six deaths and all of your children dying before you. That would mean breaking your heart over and over. It was physically painful for me to know this would now remain my reality.

I then forgave myself, forgave the others, and thanked the powers that be for the revelations of consciousness and my ability to transform and heal myself. I became thankful for the pain because without the pain, I would not have known there was an issue. I began to see that my soul needed this awareness for healing, and I forgave my naivety and re-found my primal innocence as the pain began to lessen and I could breathe again. This lifetime is not one for a family with birthed children because I know I need more time for self-discovery. It will be as it is meant to be, and so it is....

What tragic event has happened in your life that has caused you to shift into a place of healing? What would it take for you finally to shift out of the place of pain and find self-love? Your wounds are not who you are. They may give you character, but they don't have to define you. When you step away from simply being a survivor of your wounds and choose to become the hero, you step into your healed self and lose your ego. What would it take for you to see yourself as a hero? What would it take to get out of the business of the mind and the stories told to yourself? Do you have practices to aid you in your healing?

"You only lose what you cling to."

— Gautama Buddha

The Buddhist Perspective of Personal Responsibility

In a nutshell, Buddhism is a philosophy of total personal responsibility. Buddha cautioned about the danger of fashioning our beliefs based on another's word or experiences. Instead, if we maintain an open mind and thoroughly investigate our own experience of life, and then we see for ourselves that a particular view agrees with both experience and reason, and that view leads to the happiness of all, then we should accept that view and live up to it! His teaching focused on the reality of human suffering and the urgent need to find lasting relief from all forms of discontent and put sufferers on a path to true happiness through enlightenment. The Buddha pointed out that no God or priest, nor any other kind of being, has the power to interfere in the working out of someone else's actions. Buddhism, therefore, teaches people to take full responsibility for themselves, their future, and their wellbeing. It was time for me truly to own my own healing; up until then, part of me was still seeking another's approval, another's expressed sorrow for my pain, or someone else to lay out the path I should follow. Looking into other belief systems helped me to step deeper into my healed self than I had ever done before. I was, after all, responsible for my own wellbeing. Ask yourself—have you truly taken responsibility for your own wellbeing? Truly? What steps have you taken?

The mind is believed to be the creator of sickness, health, and all of our problems. The cause of disease is believed to be internal, not external. All of our positive, negative, or neutral actions create imprints on our mind and have the potential to appear at some time in the future. Negative actions can surface at any time in the form of problems or sickness; the positive ones surface in the form of happiness, health, or success. The basic root of problems and sickness is selfishness; it's said to be the inner enemy. Selfishness causes engagement in negative actions, which places negative imprints on the mind. These negative actions can be of body, speech, or mind and appear as jealousy, anger, and greed. These feelings in turn result in a mind without peace. On the other hand, thoughts and actions directed to the wellbeing of others bring happiness and peace to the mind. Developing compassion is more important than having friends, wealth, or education. Only compassion guarantees a happy and peaceful mind. We can use our sickness and problems in a very powerful way for spiritual growth, resulting in the development of compassion and wisdom.

To heal present sickness, we have to engage in positive actions now. To prevent sickness from occurring again in the future, we have to purify, or clear, the negative karmic imprints that remain. Karma is the creator of all happiness and suffering. If we don't have negative karma, we will not get sick or receive harm from others. Buddhism asserts that everything that happens to us now is the result of our previous actions, not only in this lifetime but in other lifetimes. What we do now determines what will happen to us in the future. It requires constant mindfulness and awareness of all the actions of our body, speech, and mind, and we should avoid actions that are harmful to ourselves and to others. Buddha said the urgent need of our existence is to find lasting relief from recurrent suffering, which robs us of happiness and leaves us in strife. We have the ability to control our destiny, including the state of our bodies and minds. In order to heal the mind, and hence the body, we have to eliminate negative thoughts and their imprints, and replace them with positive thoughts and imprints. When we do that, it is believed that each one of us has unlimited potential. The Buddha taught that before we can understand life and death, we must understand the self. If we can see through the delusion of the small, individual self, we experience that which is not subject to birth and death.

"No one saves us but ourselves.
No one can and no one may.
We ourselves must walk the path."

— Gautama Buddha, Sayings of Buddha

Following are the central teachings of the Buddha, around which all other teachings revolve:

Four Noble Truths:

1. **First Noble Truth:** All forms of being, human and otherwise, are afflicted with suffering.

2. **Second Noble Truth:** The cause of this suffering is craving. We continually search for something outside ourselves to make us happy. But no matter how successful we are, we never remain satisfied.

3. **Third Noble Truth:** Through diligent practice, we can put an end to craving in the experience of enlightenment, which is the complete letting go of the illusion of soul, all consequent desire, and aversion—leading to enlightenment (*bodhi*, "awakened"). The enlightened being exists in a state called *Nirvana*.

4. **Fourth Noble Truth:** Peaceful and blissful enlightenment is achieved through a gradual training. There is no particular benefit to merely believing in a doctrine. Instead, the emphasis is on living the doctrine and walking the path. This is called the Middle Way or the Eightfold Path.

The Eightfold Path:

The path is quite deep, so I won't get that detailed here. But the path is divided into three main sections: wisdom, ethical conduct, and mental discipline. They can be roughly understood as the following:

Wisdom: Right View and Right Intention are the wisdom path. Right View is not about believing in doctrine, but in perceiving the true nature of ourselves and the world around us. Right Intention refers to the energy and commitment we need to be fully engaged in Buddhist practice.

Ethical Conduct: Right Speech, Right Action, and Right Livelihood are the ethical conduct path. They call us to take care in our speech, our actions, and our daily lives to do no harm to others and to cultivate wholesomeness in ourselves.

Mental Discipline: Through Right Effort, Right Mindfulness, and Right Concentration, we develop the mental discipline to cut through delusion. Many schools of Buddhism encourage seekers to meditate to achieve clarity and focus of mind.

We may perceive the pain of our past actions and wounds as too far in the past to think we can do anything about them, or they may be so much a part of your present that it seems unlikely they will pass or heal, but what truly only matters is the now. How you reason these issues in the mind has everything to do with how your life goes from this point forward. From this time, right here and now, you can choose to step into your authentic power and into your becoming.

Tips for Stepping Into Your Becoming:
(From Japanese Buddhist, Miyamoto Musashi)

1. Accept everything just the way it is.
2. Do not seek pleasure for its own sake.
3. Do not, under any circumstances, depend on a partial feeling.
4. Think lightly of yourself and deeply of the world.
5. Be detached from desire your whole life long.
6. Do not regret what you have done.
7. Never be jealous.
8. Never let yourself be saddened by a separation.

9. Resentment and complaint are appropriate neither for our self nor others.
10. Do not let yourself be guided by the feeling of lust or love.
11. In all things, have no preferences.
12. Be indifferent to where you live.
13. Do not pursue the taste of good food.
14. Do not hold on to possessions you no longer need.
15. Do not act following customary beliefs.
16. Do not collect weapons or practice with weapons beyond what is useful.
17. Do not fear death.
18. Do not seek to possess either goods or fiefs (anything of value) for your old age.
19. Respect Buddha and the gods without counting on their help.
20. You may abandon your own body but you must preserve your honor.
21. Never stray from the Way.

EXERCISE:

What are you going to let go of from your past? ________________

____

____

____

____

____

What reflections in others are present in you that you wish to shift?

____

____

____

____

____

____

____

Note lessons you have learned in this chapter and how you are going to move forward in a more positive direction: ____________________

____

____

____

____

____

____

____

AWAKEN — TRANSFORM — REALIZE

Chapter 5

Loving Your Truth

"Three things cannot be long hidden:
the sun, the moon, and the truth."

— Buddha

God created a divine being when you were created. You are unique. Your life is purposeful. Your soul could have likely incarnated in many places, but it came here to be in the physical body you now own. You came for the experience in this skin, in the location you live, with the people you call friends and family, and for this very and exact moment that you are in right here, right now. I can't stress enough how important it is to be with what is and know or learn to love the truth of you. You matter! The purpose of life is simply to have "the experience." In the having of the experience, when we find love, we find truth, and when we find truth, we find love. This can be self-love or compassion for others, which ultimately leads us back to love. But, ultimately, it's about what's found inside of you.

No matter how you look at life, it is love that drives everything. In the loss of love, there is pain. In the misunderstanding of love, there is confusion. In the confusion, there can be anger, remorse, and countless other feelings. In war, it is love and peace we ultimately seek. No matter where you are in your life, it is love that drives the soul. When someone acts out, he generally does so for acknowledgement—to be seen or loved. And when someone is seeking love, he generally hasn't found it in self. Life and finding love and truth is a journey.

The depth of love a soul knows is achieved through a learned process, and the ultimate love doesn't come from another person, but from within. We are not on this planet alone. Every interaction with each unique person or experience is meant, ultimately, for growth of the soul toward self truth, universal truth, or love. Finding your inner truth and coming to peace with it may mean you have reached a certain level of self-love. It's really all quite circular if you think about it.

If love is the ultimate truth, why are we not taught about it? Where can you go to find love? I spent many years seeking love from others and treating myself poorly in the process. I sought to find love in a stressful career, in dating, in a failed marriage, in materialistic binge purchases, and everywhere across the world—everywhere outside of myself. But love can be better found in the comfortable and uncomfortable moments with self. Ultimately, love is what yoga teaches—the mastery of self. Work yourself through pain and feel accomplishment. Rise above pain and challenges, whether they be emotional or physical, and become a master of self. Becoming a master of self allows us to become teachers to help others rise into self-mastery.

Each new life experience comes on God's divine timeline. Having achieved a level of self-mastery allows faith, and within faith is freedom. Countless people have come to me over the years telling me they needed a healing session because they were seeking freedom. I often wondered, freedom from what? Freedom from self? Many other people I have known have moved to new locations and hoped for fresh starts, but the same problems kept occurring. A move doesn't always change patterns or behaviors. You still follow yourself. If you cannot escape yourself, then the best way to find freedom is to find a way to love yourself, to think of yourself as sacred and special—such thoughts do not come from a place of the ego, but as a reflection of the divine. Speak highly of yourself, to yourself, and allow the divine to shine through. To better love yourself, cultivate compassion for yourself. You can achieve that by turning inward and using meditation.

One of the most commonly taught forms of Buddhist meditation is the *metta* (loving-kindness) meditation. This practice dates back more than 2,500 years. Finding any image that inspires feelings of love, compassion, and warmth as an object of compassion is the first step. Once compassion is cultivated, it can be turned inward to your self. Have compassion for your inner critic. Once you find compassion for yourself, you will find self-love. I'll show you this meditation in Chapter 10.

When the world says, "Give up,"
Hope whispers, "Try it one more time."

— Author Unknown

Being White Light

I believe the purpose of physical life is about the experience and the attitude we have going through those experiences. I've talked to many who believe the purpose is love, but I think that's just one component. Clearly, a lot had to happen to come into this physical form, so it must be purposeful. Perhaps it's not just about living a purposeful life, but also about how we treat our self and others, and how we go about finding out who we are meant to be or what we are meant to do as we live purposefully. But what does all that have to do with stepping into your becoming?

Think back to your childhood; what did you really love or what were you really good at doing at a young age? When you were a little boy or girl and someone asked you what you were going to be when you grew up, what did you say? In those new moments on our planet, you had a closer connection to the spiritual realm you more recently came from. Getting an idea of what you wanted to be can provide some direction to why you came, but I believe it's only part of the experience. We didn't just come to be something or gain a title. But it can sometimes help provide a sense of direction and purpose. If we came simply for the experience, then whatever title we call ourselves by doesn't really matter. Does our soul contain the blueprint for being a particular title? Or does it contain the ingredients simply to be? Perhaps the bigger accomplishment is just the ability to be.

What if just being was enough? What if in just existing, you were accomplishing all you needed to do and be? If that was simply it, then maybe I could stop writing, and you could stop reading, and we could both just be, right? Well, perhaps. What if money and material things didn't matter, and roles and titles didn't matter, and the real challenge was just to be and have the experience? Maybe it would be better to do so with a positive outlook and with a heart full of love verses anger? Maybe we come into the physical because we need to feel emotion and our bodies? And maybe we need to get through the challenges of embodiment and find ourselves and the divine? And then once we do, we can help others find their essence of self and how it relates to the divine.

When I was growing up, most people thought I wanted to be an artist. But what I wanted to be was more than that—it just was not something I could explain to others. It was simply white light. I knew I was meant to be white light. How do you explain that? And maybe I wanted to be an artist or builder of white light? But who does that? It would take me years to understand what this really meant. But as life progressed, it became easier to understand. I knew I was not meant to be any one thing. I was not necessarily meant to have a title. I was not even meant really to be any of the roles I played in my careers, but I *was* meant to have the experiences. The experiences in my careers formed me into the person I am today, not the titles I had. I lost many jobs and bounced around to many others trying to find happiness…to find myself. I was always frustrated in my career because I could just never find the white light or the right fit. I would try out my career like trying on a pair of poorly fitting blue jeans. I'd put one leg in, and it seemed like it would fit. Then I'd put in the next and I'd say, "Okay, I've got this." Then I'd pull them up and they were always too tight, confining, and uncomfortable. And seriously, I have never found a pair of jeans to be comfortable anyway. Did that mean I was a failure because my jeans didn't fit? I think not.

We can get hard on ourselves about all the things we perceive to be our failures in life, but I have a saying: *"I haven't failed at anything. I just haven't succeeded at something I wasn't meant to do in the first place."* After so much heartache in my life for so many years, I started to shift my thinking. I started to see that if I could triumph over the things I thought I was failing at, then wasn't I actually succeeding? I wondered further and began to see that there really is no such thing as failure. The real issue was the idea that I had failed. It was what was in my mind. How my mind functioned was what was failing. If I believed I had failed, well…then I had.

Depression in Community

Life challenges can lead you into your truth and help you develop a deeper love for self. At several points in my life, I would diagnose myself as depressed. I never opted to take drugs or even see a professional because I saw depression as something I didn't need help with but something I needed to work myself through. I'm a hands-on kind of person, and I don't generally ask for help. Something in me told me that if I could only get through this phase, I wouldn't have to go through it again. I wanted single-handedly to conquer my self and master this depression.

I developed this hands-on attitude about life after just one time trying to hire a general contractor to install a patio door for me, believe it or not. I had to take time off work to meet a sales guy, but, of course, he didn't show up and had to reschedule. I needed to take more time off work to meet him again. Then when the time to do the work came, the wrong door was ordered. If you're a homeowner, you've likely experienced this same situation. The contractor told me he would give me a discount if I chose to install it. I was young and broke so I agreed. It turns out this was not only the start of a love-affair with home remodeling, but an opportunity to learn how to do projects like this myself. Plus, I knew no one cared about my house as much as me so I saw this as an opportunity to do a better job myself. (Perhaps this was an early lesson in looking after my own personal house of mind, body, and spirit?) I developed an attitude and a saying: "If someone else can do this, I can do it better!" This attitude became a part of my thinking when life got challenging, too. I saw that I could have other people help me with things, but I wouldn't be truly satisfied until I at least tried it myself first. When it came to my depression, it was no different.

Being depressed is a funny thing. When you're not happy you attract more reasons not to be happy, and more unhappy people choose to surround you. Then, before you know it, you are in deep. I studied my depression for many years, and I watched it and learned from it. When I began my shamanic studies, I learned even more about it. But it wasn't until years down the road and with many heartaches under my belt that I began to find something rather interesting. I was in spiritual communities I thought were supposed to be good for my soul, uplift me, and educate me on how to be a better person, and in many cases they did, but they were also filled with other people who had lots of problems, all seeking solutions.

One Christmas, I decided I was too depressed to spend time with family, so I drove to a yoga event in Florida with a guy I was dating. Not only were we both miserably sick with sinus infections the entire time, but we were surrounded by people who were also boycotting the season and their families. Christmas had always been my favorite time of year, but this year I was feeling depressed and didn't want to pretend I was happy. However, I didn't plan to go to avoid my family and the spirit of the season. I began to miss my family, the spirit, the smells of fresh foods, and even a bit of the materialism, décor, and gift-giving, which was kind of a taboo in a yoga community. I realized that I might never go to another yoga event during the holidays because it was a false substitute for the holiday season. But I did see it as a great place to be for people who had nowhere else to go. I didn't want to judge it, but it just wasn't a fit for me. It did teach me what I didn't like, which helped to clarify for me what I did like.

Many spiritual communities tell you to follow the teachings, not the teacher. Some practitioners don't hear the message and follow the teacher regardless; others can't see beyond the teachings and get stuck, being unable to open to alternative ways. Learning to follow your own self-guidance (with or without a certain level of instruction) can be very empowering. It's time to take the training wheels off and ride the bike! Regardless of who is present in these communities—see the teachings first. See the reflection of who is being mirrored back to you, and allow for the healing and transformation to happen without judgment as you discover the like within you. I have found more healers needing healing in healing classes than healers who help others heal! I've found more close-minded spiritual people with ideological beliefs in spiritual communities than those who are supposed to be "just average people." I've had spiritual friends who didn't want to be friends with people who didn't go through similar indoctrinations into their particular method of practice, healing, or spiritual rituals or beliefs. And when you are working as a healer, you attract those needing to be healed in every avenue of your life. People with severe problems want to be "fixed" instead of being shown how to heal themselves. It all grinded on my psyche and enhanced my depression.

As I studied depression, I realized it often consists of a kind of righteous attitude that things should go a certain way. It's up there with anger, and both are self-indulgent. And if something needs "fixing," then you're kind of saying God's creation doesn't meet your standards. In the place of expectation, many things can fall short. When something wasn't going the way I had hoped, I would feel helpless and not in control of my own path. It would take me some time to realize I was not in control of much of my path in the physical world I had incarnated into. But using my intuitive and psychic gifts, I would sense that only a part of me had incarnated into this physical body and another part (or parts) of me existed elsewhere, in another dimension or maybe even a parallel universe. I would sense that a larger part of me was guiding me. I was only a small essence of me.

If I were to believe this, it meant I needed faith that I was ultimately guiding my earth body, mind, and spirit. Was there room to be depressed if a larger part of me was involved in helping steer the direction of this earth life? Was I beginning to see the divine within me? Did I place myself in the situations that were mirroring back aspects of my depressed self? And why would I do that? There had to be a reason. I became a curious student of my own depression. I studied the patterns and behaviors of self until my essence began to peer through.

Finding Your Essence

Your essence is your soul, spirit, nature, core, or whatever term you want to use to define your true substance. Essence is also your style and how you express yourself. Your essence drives you and it's what your spirit revolves around. To embrace the essence of self, we must never work against our self. If I were to use the reflection around me to identify who I am, would I be able to understand my essence? Could I alter it? Can we become lost in the stories around us and loose our essence? Or could we use our essence to find or love our truth?

Perhaps I was looking for the negative rather than the positive? What if I simply stepped away from judgment and watched the reflection rather than finding fault with it? And what if I found all the beautiful qualities in my environment and focused on them rather than on what was wrong?

In my place of depression and in my healing and spiritual environments, it seemed like I was being shown or observing only what needed to be "fixed" versus what was perfect exactly as it was. What if a simple shift in my thinking could change my perception? What if we sought help in others, or worked as healers for others, to help see the light within versus all the lifetimes of pain and wrongs? Why was everyone in every community I was involved in focused on pain and wrongs? Or was it just me? Was that just my reflection? What if stepping into our becoming didn't involve a title or a job but involved shifting into a new consciousness? What if I stepped outside of all the stories? Would discovering my essence unravel the mysteries of my actions and explain my mistakes? And shoot, were there even such things as mistakes? Perhaps I could find more grace and clarify my choices? If I could begin to see the essence of others and life around me, perhaps I could flow with it better. Would I then be able to connect with the world in a deeper manner? If I could relate with each living being better rather than working against it, I would be able to shift everything that was intersecting in my own life in a positive (or perhaps even more neutral) way.

Finding Aloha

In the aloha spirit of the Hawaiian islands, this would mean that everything was, in essence, perfect as it was, without our human judgment. Being in aloha means being aware that I am part of all and all is part of me. Pain and joy are shared. There is a respect for all that is a part of the Creator. It's a kind of oath that all creation takes that no person or thing will be harmed. When something is taken, it is asked for first and the need is explained and often something is left in exchange. All that is on the earth is cared for, cherished, and protected. We are all in unity and harmony with our real self, God, and mankind. We are here to share in the present joy, life energy, and breath. The Shaman of Peru refer to this as "creating our reality." In Hawaiian, aloha means much the same. You and I are a conscious creation of reality in the present moment where our reality exists. We came to cherish, protect, and take care of this being-ness on Earth. The Hawaiians believed nature was not separate from the self, and we must give ourselves back to nature. The life and death of plants sustain all creatures by providing food and medicine. The gift of life passes from human to plants and then back to humanity. It is believed that we can discover the nature of our existence here on earth in the nature of our land. It is believed we can gain wisdom from the wind, water, soil, and trees.

When I was studying Peruvian Shamanism, I was taught the basis for these Hawaiian ways, but stepping into the way of the aloha spirit and the Hawaiian culture would enhance this learning. It's much easier to hold a neutral mind in nature because we are captured by its beauty. Only when nature is destroyed by man do we generally judge. But we are more or less put into our place when Mother Nature shows us her strength. If we are truly one with nature, then the idea of "having a dark cloud over our heads" could have much more meaning than we know. I personally have noticed that the closer I have gotten with nature, the more it seemed to mimic my emotions. I taught a weekly yoga class for many years, and it was one of the happiest days of the week for me. It always seemed to be raining on these days. It didn't just sprinkle, but it generally was a downpour! If it were too cold for rain, it snowed. So my question would be: How can we collaborate with nature in order to calm the earth? As we discover our essence, can we really make a shift? I believe so.

Just living is not enough, said the butterfly.
One must have sunshine, freedom, and a little flower.

— Hans Christian Andersen

Loving Your Truth means accepting yourself as you are. It doesn't mean you can't change who you are at this moment, but it does mean having a deep love for yourself. When you love the truth of who you are at this very moment, it means you understand there is room for improvement, but it doesn't mean you hate the person you are in the meantime. It means you have accepted what might have been previously thought of as your faults or areas where you had self-blame and you have found a level of forgiveness in the perceived wrongdoings of your past or confusion about your future. There is a force within us that has a desire to thrive, to thrive in being truly who we are and who we are meant to be. How are you going to have this life's experience? Are you going to thrive and step into your truth, or are you going to live a life of always questioning your contribution to the world?

Tips for Stepping Into Your Becoming:

1. The purpose of life is simply to have "the experience."
2. Have the experience with the right attitude.
3. You haven't failed at anything you weren't meant to do.
4. Live fully in your essence.
5. You were meant to thrive.

EXERCISE:

Who or what has opened your heart to the depth of love? Can you open deeper? ____

____

____

When do you talk negatively to yourself the most? What do you say? Can you correct that negative self-talk and what could you say instead? ____

____

____

What did you most want to do or be when you were a child? How does that relate to what you are doing now? Is what you are doing now contrary to your true essence? _________________________

____

____

____

____

AWAKEN — TRANSFORM — REALIZE

Chapter 6

The Nature of Nature Consciousness

"All creatures in the universe
return to the point where they began.
Returning to the source is tranquility,
meaning submitting to what is and what is to be."

— *Tao Te Ching, Verse 16*

I believe that stepping into our becoming requires us to be more conscious and to be aware of the greater consciousness that exists on our planet. We tend to focus on human consciousness and miss the bigger picture. Let me explain how that bigger picture of universal consciousness affects all of us.

New research is coming out revealing the living consciousness of plants. They are aware and are communicating. Plants can sense light and grow toward it. They can also "smell" chemicals released by other plants and that triggers specific reactions. It has even been found that plants can "hear." I read recently that even playing the sound of a caterpillar munching on leaves to plants causes them to release defensive chemicals. It has even been found that plants can form memories and react to someone who has done harm to them. New research shows that trees in a forest ecosystem are interconnected through an underground network; not only do they exchange nutrients, but older trees transfer knowledge to the younger trees and animals in the forest. Larger, older "mother trees" are serving as hubs to the younger ones. It's now being said that one plus one equals more than two in the forest. They are communicating with each other to survive. When deforestation happens the trees don't get to transfer their knowledge and knowledge is lost.

I've been a veg-head (vegan/vegetarian) for twenty-five years. I opted not to eat animals because I love them too much to harm them. I went a period of time thanking plants for growing just for me to eat, and recognized the love they must have to provide for us. I even had a hard time eating them knowing I was ingesting a living being and consciously ending its life in doing so. I went for months fasting, eating, and then crying when I did eat. Eventually I came to a place of being overly thankful and having a psychic conversation with fruit or vegetables. I wanted to understand their level of consciousness more. I even did a Shamanic Ayahuasca ceremony at one point to learn about the plant medicine of the Andes in South America and how it was said to be a teacher, but it took me a while to realize how much deeper it could go. There are so many reasons to go vegan, but isn't consciousness, consciousness?

I wrestled with the idea that I would feed my dogs an animal that was killed in order for them to survive; I thought it unfair to choose one over another. I concluded that in order to have a fur kid that prefers to eat another animal, I would essentially have to kill for it. I tried feeding them vegan meals on countless occasions, but their health suffered from it. They lost hair, and then they soon wouldn't eat. The reality here is that there is no difference in consciousness whether I kill a plant for my dinner or feed my dogs a chicken for theirs. How do we choose one life over another? Survival requires these difficult choices, but the choices can be made with reverence and prayer. If we eat an animal that was brutally murdered, we can grow sick eating it. We can take on its karma. We can take on its fears. And if a plant secretes a toxin prior to us ingesting it, we can take on those toxins or fears in our bodies. A process is needed for releasing the fear, pain, and negative factors in our food's cellular memory. If we adopted prayer, could we release these issues before ingesting the food? Where is the line drawn between harm and the need for survival? Can we simply just be thankful and have reverence? And if food is not killed in violent ways, but done with reverence, can it be prepared with energy that is not detrimental to our health? Are you thankful for the entire process of how each meal ended up on your plate? The growers, the harvesters, the sellers all imprint an energy on your meal. Perhaps we can use the Hawaiian methods of prayer if we have no others. "I love you. I am sorry. Please forgive me. Thank you."

"Changing is not just changing the things outside of us. First of all we need the right view that transcends all notions including of being and non-being, creator and creature, mind and spirit. That kind of insight is crucial for transformation and healing."

— Thich Nhat Hanh

Every thing and every being on our planet is connected. Not one being is superior to another, but as humans, we sometimes forget that the life of an ant, butterfly, or spider is equally important. I always feel bad when someone kills a bug that entered his or her home because nature was here first, and the bug was just trying to survive or maybe just took a wrong turn. We can see a bigger picture than they can, so shouldn't we help them back outside? We know from science that carnivores eat herbivores, eliminating nutrient rich waste that nourishes the plants. Bacteria process waste to enrich plants which nourish the herbivores. Flowing rivers are stripped of nutrients as they pass through the roots of plants before entering the pristine reefs that nourish the sea creatures. We ward off viruses, bacteria, and disease by ingesting the exoskeletons of coral animals and sea creatures. No matter where we look in the chain of sustenance, we see how life is fundamentally intertwined. *The Tao de Ching*, an ancient Chinese book whose title translates as "The Classic of the Virtuous Way," refers to this process as the path of least resistance, we allow life to take its course *naturally,* without interference. Exerting the will against events will only create further obstruction in the river of life.

Therefore, I believe that stepping into our becoming means stepping into a more conscious awareness of what and who surrounds us and letting all of it flow in a natural process. When you contemplate the concept of consciousness, you begin to see that as humans we came to earth from some other spiritual realm with the idea we would lose some or all of our consciousness. Perhaps part of our life's purpose is to work to regain our consciousness partially or fully as we progress through this earth life? Do we need to lose ourselves to find our true natures? How does nature take a role in finding our human nature? According to the earliest Taoist texts, when human nature is aligned with the rest of nature, order and harmony are the result.

At the moment, we can't get to other planets to live. We might be able to travel to them in our mind's eye, but not physically. And if we did, we wouldn't be able to live there. We have no other choice but to live here. I used to get really deep and dreamy about other worlds and spiritual beings, and I would go to extreme depths to understand how to talk to an angel, an alien, a fairy, a lost loved one. I did anything and everything to talk to anyone who existed, more or less, in a fantasy land other than here. Then I realized how important it was to be a physical being because I had left the spirit world to be here. I must have felt the need to be here. Why did I leave that realm to come to earth and be carbon-based? And why was I so desperately trying to connect to someone or something else? Taoists believe our goal as humans is to experience a long and healthy life. But we can deviate from the natural order and bring destruction upon ourselves and those around us. If a person of impeccable character leads with integrity, then others will naturally follow that example.

Our earth is so beautiful and both so strong and so fragile. When you choose to take on the care of an animal or a plant, you begin to see how reliant they are on you, how fragile, how much they count on you and your decisions on their behalf. But you also see how strong they function together. The Dalai Lama said:

"By simply looking at these innocent animals, insects, ants, bees,

etc. quite often I develop some kind of respect for them. How? Because they have no religion, no constitution, no police force, nothing. But they live in harmony through the natural law of existence or nature's law or system."

Cherishing Others More than Self

The Dalai Lama believes that, as humans, we tend to go against basic human nature. We could survive without religion or government, but not without human affection. Affection is the key to a good heart. Great compassion is generated in dependence upon each and every single obscured, suffering, sentient being. Loving an animal, for example, is said to show practitioners how they must cherish others more than the self. There is no way we can harm sentient beings. It is impossible to get angry with them; it is impossible to criticize them; it is impossible to harm them in any way. An advanced practitioner (bodhisattva) will feel about sentient beings the way a mother feels about her beloved child. She cherishes them more than her life itself. A bodhisattva cherishes sentient beings most, doing everything for sentient beings. Therefore, a mosquito (or another person) is most cherished by a bodhisattva. A bodhisattva does everything, including attaining the path to enlightenment, *for* this sentient being. And if you can give some small comfort to this other being, that's what brings the most happiness. It is believed that when you create good karma by helping others to have a long life, you too have a long life. And liberating animals is one of the best means to bring peace in this world—for the animals and the human. Even people with life-threatening illnesses have recovered this way. *Dogs, for example, are considered to be very special because some Buddhist traditions believe they are monks or nuns who broke their vows in their previous lives and are living this life out as dogs.*

Thousands of years ago, the Taoists developed their philosophies based on nature's ways:

All things mutually involve each other.
At the root of our experiences are clues to our evolutionary journey.
In this, you can become the master of your experiences.

These masters observed the synergistic way that all things move together; they came to know that life's regenerative changing events unleash "te," which is "the natural power in me." They said that all things in nature have a purpose, and we need only open to our purposeful life. An individual who is open to the changes discovers how life keeps us authentic and open to growth.

With a sense of trust, the outer world mysteriously changes. To the ancient Taoist, nature was a teacher. The masters studied natural processes to understand the human condition. Observing how nature silently produced the myriad of plant and animal life without apparent effort, the masters applied this same sense of ease to daily life. When cultivated alongside of fearlessness, te is like water that finds its own course, without any sense of barriers. Water can dissolve mountains, and it evens out, regardless of where it flows. The power of te connects us with the germinating power of life.

Transcending the gate or "the illusion of obstacles," leads to a type of paradise in consciousness, a place without boundaries. A change in perspective allows us to see obstacles in a great river that only moves forward. And even when we fail at something, we are left with what is necessary for our growth. Thus, we never really fail. When we re-evaluate the obstacle: "dimly visible, it only seemed as if it were there." It is natural to take action and act with original sincerity with a response that is cultivated in solitude, rather than through others' responses. This ensures that we meet with no resistance as we travel through the "river of life."

The Taoist masters say the te is the creative power that comes from spontaneous and natural expression. If the character is authentic, we become, quite by accident, authentically effective. "Because this power is most true, within it there is confidence." This confidence creates the magnetism that makes a great leader.

As you begin to heal and transform yourself, you are able to begin opening up to the idea of being able to heal others, live for others, and step deeply into self-love along the way. Love and compassion become the truth of all of existence. When life beats you down, by walking any spiritual path in search of self or awareness, conquering any adversity with consciousness, putting in earth time and years, the mind becomes less of a nuisance and you begin to see that you have awakened, transformed, and started to gain glimpses of the you that you can become. And through that realization, you become more compassionate and caring, and you see the connectedness to supporting and loving others. This is not just great for the self, but it's great for conscious business practices, conscious living, and conscious being.

Tips for Stepping Into Your Becoming:

1. See the other as you.
2. Become aware of your reflection in your surroundings and shift into the person you want to see in the world. If you don't like what

you see around you, change it! Change you!

3. Step out of your story and heal with awareness.
4. Don't beat yourself up as you work through your life stories.
5. Be thankful for your wounds. They show you how to improve.
6. Respect all that is a part of the creator.
7. Love other more than self.
8. Allow nature to show you the way.
9. Be spontaneous and express yourself naturally.
10. Follow the path of least resistance.

EXERCISE:

When you speak to another person and provide him or her with directions on what to do next, do you take your own advice? Catch yourself each time you say, "You should do…" and then ask yourself what you should be doing for you. Make notes here. ____________

When you talk about healing or empowering yourself, what stories do you get caught up in about why you can't? ____________________

What do you perceive to be your wounds? How can you be thankful for them? ____________________

Walk into nature and just observe for a month. Take notes here on your observations. ______________________________________

When you have to make a decision in your life, try this approach: Go with the most simple. Try it for a few days and then ask yourself, "How is this working for me?" ______________________________

PART 3

REALIZE

Self-realization is defined as "fulfillment by oneself of the possibilities of one's character or personality." Yogananda defined self-realization as "the knowing—in body, mind, and soul—that we are one with the omnipresence of God; that we do not have to pray that it come to us, that we are not merely near it at all times, but that God's omnipresence is our omnipresence; that we are just as much a part of Him now as we ever will be. All we have to do is improve our knowing."

He who realizes his self,
comes to know the essence.

— *Guru Nanak*

Self-realization is acknowledged in Hinduism, Buddhism, Sikhism, and in Western psychology. It is related to self-actualization, enlightenment, and non-dualism. For the Hindu, it has a large presence. It teaches self-realization is knowledge of the true self beyond both delusion and identification with material phenomena. It refers to self-identification and not ego identification. It is said to be achieved through four types of spiritual practice: karma yoga (action), Raja yoga (meditation), Bhakti yoga (for devotion), and Jnana yoga (knowledge). (NOTE: Kundalini Yoga incorporates Bhakti yoga, Shakti yoga [for power], and Raja yoga for mental power and control–practicing to liberate oneself from one's karma and to realize one's dharma or life purpose.) It is also taught with Sahara yoga, devotional Advaita,

and by Ramana Maharshi. Buddhism teaches awakening but not so much the existence of a separate self. Sikhism teaches the purifying of self from the false ego.

In the West, self-realization was discussed by Freud as self-understanding, Carl Jung discussed it as individualism and a shifting from the ego to self. And many others spoke of it as psychological growth, the awakening and manifestation of the ethical, esthetic, and religious experiences and activities. But overall, it's based on Eastern spirituality, and the West is still growing in its understanding. At its core, self-realization is the ultimate goal of a human being, attaining permanent happiness and complete independence and freedom from worldly bondage.

It is generally viewed that true happiness results from self-realization.

AWAKEN — TRANSFORM — REALIZE

Chapter 7

Learning Happiness from the Masters

"Happiness is essentially a state of going somewhere, whole heartedly, one-directionally, without regret or reservation."

— William H. Sheldon

Happiness begins with commitment within yourself—a certain way of behavior within yourself. Developing a meditation practice to absorb the divine and neutralize yourself is a great place to start. Make it a routine. Commit to being a kind person. Keep your heart open. Watch your words and your actions. When you act, act with compassion. Do the thing that must be done with love in your heart, even if it's challenging.

Kundalini Yoga and Yogi Bhajan

It's been stated in the practice of Kundalini yoga that when your character becomes solid within yourself, people know they can trust you. Your character becomes your projection and that gives you dignity. God then acts through you and you act with a sense of sacredness. But, when you become God for another person (you put yourself on the line for someone else), you become divine and you recognize the divine within yourself. That commitment gives you grace. Kundalini yoga is a tool to anchor and center yourself to hold your grace. The power to sacrifice is when you are not busy living within yourself (your head) but you live in your heart (where God lives). God lives in your heart and presides over your head. Don't let your mind tell you stories. Sit in the light of God. The moment of sacrifice is only a moment, and no person can take your happiness away. You will begin to feel thankful for your commitment, character, dignity, and grace.

Much like the Dalai Lama's beliefs around compassion, happiness is the result of developing our consciousness and personality, and when we enter the state of happiness, then we are capable of living for each other. Happiness is not necessarily about satisfying our own desires. We are the happiest when we can uplift another person or a difficult situation. This view of life comes when we trust in our own relationship to the Infinite. Kundalini yoga works to develop human sensitivity and human vastness. In this opening, we begin to experience our lives as part of an endless giving cycle. We give to others. The Infinite gives to us. There is no lack, no fear, and no reaction. Happiness comes from being in that flow. Yogi Bhajan said that happiness is a birthright. In the Kundalini yoga lifestyle, there are specific steps to happiness, and each step is said to build upon the next.

The Seven Steps to Happiness

1. **Commitment**: The first step is commitment. In every life you are meant to commit. That is why the word is commit-meant. Commitment gives you CHARACTER.

2. **Character**: Character is when all your characteristics—all facets, flaws, and facts—are under your control. Yin and yang meet there, totally balanced. Character gives you DIGNITY.

3. **Dignity**: People start trusting you, liking you, respecting you. Dignity will give you DIVINITY.

4. **Divinity**: What is Divinity? Divinity is when people have no duality about you. They trust you right away. They have no fear about you. Divinity gives you GRACE.

5. **Grace**: Where there is grace, there is no interference, no gap between two people, no hidden agenda. Grace gives you the power to SACRIFICE.

6. **Power to Sacrifice**: You can stand any pain for that person. That sacrifice gives you HAPPINESS.

Happiness:

"Commitment—the power to succeed when you are powerless.
Character—you cannot be shaken.
Dignity—do not hesitate to do what you have to do for somebody.
Divinity—nothing can touch you.
Grace—stand any disgrace with grace.

Power to sacrifice—know you own nothing, that everything is of God, and give to whomsoever has the need.
Happiness—do something for no self-gain.
A few breaths of life through you can uplift something for a moment.
"I" has only one meaning—that you can do something for somebody.
When "I" is for yourself, you have wasted your life."

— *Yogi Bhajan*

Yogi Bhajan used to say: "If you can't find God in yourself, you cannot find God at all." When you really begin to see God, you are beyond the sensory. You must find your own identity and truth within. We are trained to find God outside of ourselves, but the source of life is within the breath. Breath is life. You only breathe when your soul is in your body. God perfected you. God is within you. God is also outside of you. God is all around you. God is not coming to save you. God gave you the strength to find self-love and to save yourself.

When you find your own soul, then you have found your soulmate. Your soul is the source of your life. God will not be an outsider once you find your soul. And once you have found it, you have found love.

You don't have to prove your love to be happy or find happiness. Love is an experience of our self within our self, the unspoken word; it is unconditional, not "If you love me, then…." Love is self-beauty and self-enlightenment, beyond God, and not limited.

The Dalai Lama

"Love and compassion are necessities, not luxuries. Without them, humanity cannot survive."

— Dalai Lama XIV, *The Art of Happiness*

The master of happiness is the Dalai Lama. He believes that happiness is the purpose of life and that no human being wants to suffer. He believes we need to develop love and compassion to get to inner tranquility. And the more we care for the happiness of others, the greater our own sense of wellbeing becomes. The Dalai Lama believes that we all undergo suffering to some degree, but it is important to understand that we do not suffer alone, and that with each struggle, we have an opportunity to improve our minds. If we gradually strive to become more compassionate and develop genuine sympathy for others' suffering, we will remove their pain, and as a result, we will increase our own serenity and inner strength.

Because the need for love lies at the very foundation of human existence, we all must depend upon the support of others at various points in life. Without proper interaction between the oceans, clouds, forests, and flowers that surround us, everything would decay. We need to have a genuine and sincere concern for others' welfare. The Dalai Lama has noted that when someone speaks with human feeling, we enjoy listening to that person, and we respond accordingly; then the whole conversation becomes interesting, however unimportant the topic may be. From the least to the most important event, the affection and respect of others are vital for our happiness; the need for human affection is in our very blood. The Dalai Lama believes that no one is born free from the need for love, and despite what we may sometimes believe, love and compassion are predominate in the world. He also believes that if the mind is tranquil and occupied with positive thoughts, the body will not easily fall prey to disease.

Because all human beings truly want happiness and not suffering, the Dalai Lama believes all beings are equal in both their desire for happiness and their right to obtain it. By understanding that we all share this desire, we automatically feel empathy, closeness, and a responsibility and desire to help others overcome their problems. This is just like Yogi Bhajan's belief that the other person is you. So how can we handle difficult situations? The Dalai Lama believes anger to be a sign of weakness rather than strength, and compassion is gentle and soft, but very powerful. Those who lose their patience are insecure and unstable. He believes when a problem arises, we need to remain humble, maintain a sincere attitude, and be concerned that the outcome is fair. We must maintain compassion and stand our ground without anger or ill-intent. Aggression and anger will only harm the other person, but we must assume the responsibility for the other person by preventing him or her from suffering and/or protecting the person from the consequences of his or her acts.

The Dalai Lama believes we must await opportunities to arrive and practice patience and goodwill. So if we truly wish to learn, we should consider our enemies to be our best teachers! He believes that for a person who cherishes compassion and love, the practice of tolerance is essential, and for that practice to occur, an enemy is indispensable. So we should feel grateful to our enemies, for it is they who can best help us to develop a tranquil mind! Also, it is often the case that enemies later become friends. But anger and hatred are our real enemies, not the people who temporarily come into our lives.

The Dalai Lama states that individual happiness can contribute in a profound and effective way to the overall improvement of our entire human community. Because we all share an identical need for love, it is possible to feel that anybody we meet, in whatever circumstances, is a brother or sister. It is foolish to dwell on external differences because our basic natures are the same. If you have a sincere and open heart, you naturally feel self-worth and confidence, so there is no need to be fearful of others. The key to a happier and more successful world is the growth of compassion. We do not need to become religious, nor do we need to believe in an ideology. All that is necessary is for each of us to develop our good human qualities.

Happiness Comes from Your Own Actions

All the power of the universe is contained in you, not outside you. God has created us. Something shaped us. Why would God make something that is good for nothing or unhappy? We waste our energy with fear, insecurity, jealousy, etc. Our words are very shallow. They should come from our heart, not our head. Learn to speak and act from the heart, and lead with commitment of character.

Happiness is when what you say and think are in harmony. It's a spiritual experience of living every moment with love, grace, and gratitude. We are basically as happy as we make up our minds to be. It is within our acceptance. Yesterday is gone, and today is here. We have the power to choose how to be. I find I wander into fear and worry sometimes by looking too far ahead, and that brings me back to the now. In the now, I ask: "Am I okay? Is my belly full? Is my bed warm? Are my dogs fed? Do I have money in my bank account?" If I can say, "Yes" to all of the above, then I say, "Then I'm okay." It's not as bad as I allow my mind to wander into. Then, when I serve others with less, I realize how much I truly do have. I watch as I give to those in need, and what no longer serves me brightens their days. If you cannot find happiness, then try volunteering. There is so much need in so many places, and in the act of giving, you will be humbled and grateful.

How do you make yourself happy? The mind has an agenda of its own, and it goes into survival mode before it is concerned with your emotional wellbeing. Become aware of the mind and the projections it makes. More self-awareness will make you more aware that your self is separate from your mind's thoughts and opinions. Your sense of fulfillment in life has very little to do with your accomplishments in the external world. Your happiness and unhappiness are created internally. If you've ever been fired from a job, you know that at first you might feel like a miserable failure. Your mind creates stories and self-criticism and blame sets in. But when time passes, you begin to see that you were simply liberated from the confines of that position, and it was a beneficial turn of events that helped you facilitate a better life. Nothing has changed over time, except for your opinions, beliefs, and mind chatter that you were or weren't a failure. In yoga, we might call this the "monkey mind." It loves to play tricks on you. Imagine shifting your opinion of the lost job immediately rather than over a period of time. Happiness and fulfillment are determined by opinions and beliefs in your own mind and can change with time and perspective. Changing your opinions, beliefs, and fears is more important than your external goals. Without the shifting of the mind, we will often be left feeling empty.

You can be a great success in your career, make lots of money, and receive awards and accolades, but if your internal world dictates that you are not enough, you will never shake these stories from your head. You must release fears, judgments, criticisms, and false beliefs. Turn your attention to changing how the virtual reality of the mind operates. You must stop the creation of the movie in your mind about the negative outcome of any situation because you will eventually create it in reality. Stop projecting scenarios. I know—that's easy to say, but changing the mind is not always easy.

The mind will go into survival mode and fight back. Recognizing your automatic reactive nature may help you to change your world. Begin to quiet the mind, its visual images and projections, and you begin to see the external world as it is. When you do, you will find out that life is even more beautiful or peaceful. The voices in your head about judgments, criticisms, fears, justifications, or even opinions and descriptions disappear. Only when you dissolve the virtual reality of your mind do you have a chance to live in the real world. In the beginning, you may only live there for a few brief moments. With practice, it will become a normal way to live. When the mind is tamed and the virtual reality dissolved, there is no longer the unhappiness, frustration, anger, or sense of emptiness. You are able to see the world as it is and people as they really are. You realize and perceive beauty as the fog lifts and your eyes open to this clarity. By dismantling the false projections of your virtual reality, you then free yourself of emotional suffering during the changing circumstances of your life.

Tips for Stepping Into Your Becoming:

1. God is within you, outside of you, is you.

2. Find compassion for another if you cannot do it for yourself.
3. Don't get angry, be thankful for an opportunity to see the true you or for change.

EXERCISE:

How many times in your life have you waited for someone else to come into your life to "save" you? Did he or she? How did you feel when no one did save you or the person you thought would save you didn't __

How do you honor yourself with self-love practices? How can you?

What can you focus on to create more greatness in your life? ____

What steps can you take to develop more compassion for others in your life? ____

What are you consciously creating in your life? ____

What do you think you might be unconsciously creating in your life?

AWAKEN — TRANSFORM — REALIZE

Chapter 8

Creating Your Reality

"We are what we think.
Everything we are arises from our thoughts.
With our thinking we create the world."

— Buddha

Dreaming Your World into Being

Many psychotherapists say that taking the time to understand your dreams allows you to take ownership of your life. When you are facing a crisis, dreams reveal the way ahead, activating self-knowledge and direction in life. Since the time of Freud and Jung, many have validated how dreams demonstrate an organizing force within the psyche. Recurring dreams may be a sign that you are not understanding some message. A few therapists have noted that once the dream is understood and the message is applied toward making changes in your life, the dream does not recur. When the dream is ignored, it becomes more aggressive and conflicted. Dreaming can even help avoid real-life crises by helping you stay on track with whatever destiny has in store for you. Dreams can function like another sensory organ, allowing you to explore your potential that transcends time and self-awareness. Taking an active approach to understanding your dreams is a process of self-enlightenment. Everything is a reflection of you. When you are stuck, a dream can show a transformative way through.

Dreams can be unique and strange, and you may not always be aware of them, but they can change you in profound ways. Brain activity rapidly increases when you are dreaming. Lucid dreaming occurs when you become conscious that you are dreaming, and suddenly, a sense of knowing you are dreaming allows you to do some fantastic things—like have the ability to fly. Many people can influence dreams in this state. When this happens, people feel more powerful because they have control over the dream—a state that translates into feeling more confident in the real world.

The ancient Taoists believed that some part of us wandered off and found enlightenment while dreaming. Chuang Tzu once dreamed he was a butterfly. When awakened, he wondered whether he was now a butterfly dreaming of being a man. Because the goal of traveling inward and observing life objectively was an important aspect of ancient Taoism, dreams were viewed as every bit as enlightening as the actual experience.

That being said, many shamanic traditions say we are all dreaming the world into being with our eyes open. We co-create reality with the help of the Universe itself. Despite what we may think, we are not the victims of a frightening creation that we're unable to influence or change. Events don't control or trap us. We must awaken to the fact that everything is a dream, and we have the ability to write a better story, one that the Universe will work to co-create with us. Whatever dream you have about yourself and the world has the ability to become reality.

Alberto Villoldo, author of *Courageous Dreaming: How Shamans Dream the World into Being*, calls this ability to co-create reality "courageous dreaming." He says we can "dream bravely" by letting go of our limiting beliefs and pushing past our fears. He says courageous dreaming allows us to create from the source where everything exists in a latent or potential state, and that physicists are now understanding that in the quantum world, nothing is "real" until it is observed.

New studies are proving what the ancient wisdom keepers of the Americas have long known. These shaman, known as the Earth Keepers, say we are dreaming the world into being through the act of simply witnessing it. The Earth Keepers know that all of creation arises from, and returns to, dreamtime. Dreamtime does not exist in a place outside of us. All matter and energy, connecting every creature, every rock, every star, and every ray of light or bit of cosmic dust, is a part of it. And the power to dream is the power to participate in creation itself. For the Earth Keepers, dreaming reality is not only a skill but a duty, one we must participate in with grace and love so our grandchildren will inherit a world where they can live in peace and abundance.

The Earth Keepers refer to an Infinite Source, or Infinity, we can only access by raising our level of consciousness. When we do so, we see we are immersed in something much larger than ourselves. Only when we experience our connection to Infinity are we able to dream powerfully. It's our sense of separation from Infinity that traps us in a place where we don't see the capacity to dream the world into being. We need to gain an understanding of our dreaming power and experience it in every cell of our bodies.

We must get beyond just the intellectual understanding of this concept or we will end up creating a far less glorious and beautiful experience of the world than we're capable of crafting. It is believed we can share the experience of Infinity right here, right now, and stop feeling disassociated and disconnected. Villoldo states that the Earth Keepers believe it takes courage to taste Infinity, but we lack courage. We have to settle for the world being dreamed by our culture or by our genes. We feel we have to settle for the nightmare. To dream courageously, we must be willing to use our heart. Otherwise, our dream will stall at the level of emotions, of thinking too much, planning too much, and worrying endlessly. Then our dream will turn into a nightmare or a mere daydream, trapping us or causing us to drift away while we wonder, "What happened?"

If dreams show us the power of the infinite nature of things, then why do we have to be asleep to notice the endless possibilities of life here and now? Perhaps we just need to release the old patterns or habits in the waking state to open up to the Infinite's endless possibilities. You have a choice in your mind between having the life you want and clinging to the reasons you can't have that life. You can have joy and peace, or you can have sorrowful memories and wounds of the past that continue to haunt you. You can have your wounds, or you can have your glory. If you want to feel empowered, you need to shift your mind and make conscious decisions to dream your world into being. The power and will is in your mind. Each thought you have creates an energy flow within and around your physical being, and it attracts its likeness. You must develop practices or techniques to learn your blocks and/or heaviness. Meditation and yoga can be great tools, but there are many others. If you attract your likeness, then you attract everything that happens in your life, whether you like to think that or not. Finding the tool(s) that works to shift your mind and your thoughts into more positive ones will change your life. The tools are numerous because we are numerous. There is no right or wrong practice or tool.

"Healing is a matter of time,
but it is sometimes also a matter of opportunity."

— Hippocrates

Getting Honest About Your Thoughts

How much chatter goes on in your head? If you are human, chatter is normal. But it is important to recognize how your low-level thoughts negatively affect your life. This is a powerful first step toward changing your experiences. Look at your energy, feelings, and thoughts about what blocks you from receiving all you desire. It is likely that by just acknowledging such thoughts and feelings, you can release them. Try not to go outside of yourself when looking for these blocks, but looking around you can be a great tool to find them, since like does attract like. Use the mirror around you to find what you wish to heal within yourself. Does it drive you crazy when your sister does A, B, or C, or your coworker does X, Y, or Z? Catch yourself when you are trying to tell another what to do. Each time you say, "You should…" is a pretty good indication of what *you* should actually be doing versus someone else.

Many times, it's the closest people in your life who irk you the most. They get under your skin because you mirror many things in each other that you wish to heal. The bigger challenge is when your partner is not willing to do the work and moves into the blame game. I went through this for years in my marriage. I was thankful for all the mirrors my husband and I held up for each other as I was awakening, but he took my commentary as blame. If your partner isn't willing to share in these moments with you, it can be challenging. It may be best to learn in a more introspective way because such lessons are ultimately for the self. I met a husband and wife once who would each acknowledge their mirror in their partner and say to each other, "Well, isn't that fascinating." Take the lesson and move on without blaming each other. I always wished for that kind of relationship. It takes cooperation and some level of awareness to have such a relationship, but it's beautiful when it happens—even if it's with family and friends.

A Course in Miracles teaches that on some level you've asked for everything that happens in your life, and your intentions create your reality. That means, we choose to experience love or fear. When we make our choice, we attract more of the same. It's not just about attracting something to make you temporarily feel better. We should focus on how we can attract more greatness into our lives and begin healing the internal condition.

You must believe that you can heal or change yourself. I have often cringed when I hear someone say she is a "cancer survivor" because she is still holding on to the cancer in some way. A person who never had cancer would never even think to use these words to identify himself as healed. And since the universe knows no negation, you must phrase your health as a present tense with no double negatives. "I am a vibrant, healthy, beautiful person." "I am a successful entrepreneur." "I am in a beautiful, loving relationship with self, a loving partner, and God." These are great statements to begin with. Sometimes, you might need acknowledgment of your wound, but let's get that acknowledgment where it's needed and move on to being vibrant!

When you go to a support group (or sometimes even a healing group), you are identifying with others in your mirror. You are what they are—be that sick, in need of healing, a drunk, a sex addict, a cancer survivor, or a sufferer. How about going out to a place filled with healthy people who are enjoying life? Listen to your intuition about what you need, and don't get caught up in a repetitive story or the story your loved one tells you. Don't let someone else's opinion of you or your wellbeing be yours. In my opinion, every physical ailment is due to a psychological imbalance, and nothing can be "caught." If you "caught a cold" from a friend or partner, it isn't really a cold. It's an opportunity to transform and heal. When you treat it like an invasion of your body and send it hate or dislike, you are really feeding it with negative mojo. You must appreciate and love it. A major illness or a simple cold generally slows you down. Get ahead of it and ask, "What are you teaching me and how can I learn more?" Play out the scenarios. Ask yourself, "If I get worse, how is this making me feel emotionally? What is this causing me to do that I wouldn't have already done?" A life-threatening disease, an ill-will friend or a judgemental family member—all great teachers! Love them and thank them, then move on.

Family members can give us so many great opportunities for self-transformation. We chose them before incarnating because we wanted teachers. So if your family gatherings are less than desirable, you may have some great opportunities for transformation if you are in a place of self-awareness rather than ego and judgment.

If a loved one is sick, ask yourself, "What about this can I love, and what is it teaching me?" See them or yourself as better—emotionally and physically. How does that look or feel? What else needs to change so you really are well? If you or a loved one are terminal, you must allow for separations and cords to be cut so that transitions can take place. Allowing the release of a loved one is very important. I've always wondered why, when someone is dying, we don't talk about the beauty of the life lived and ease that person back home. We need to allow, forgive, and love. It is selfish to want someone to stay when he or she must go back home. We are all here temporarily, and we *must* know that in every fiber of our being! Most importantly, we must surrender to the outcome. There is nothing to fear in death—there is only liberation! We tend to panic at the time of a health crisis. There comes a time to trust in the power that created you or your loved ones. Find peace, compassion, and trust in the divine. We are not the boss of God.

When we learn to get honest with our thoughts, we begin to take ownership of what they create. Our thoughts create and form our reality. Saying something and meaning it are two entirely different things. The reality is that if you keep talking about something, it is in your awareness and you've done nothing to shift your thinking, thus shifting your awareness. It is fine to be aware of your weaknesses, but don't own them in every instance in your life unless you want to create more awareness of them with others. Try a fun game and make a list of your weaknesses and create positive affirmations that counter them. Don't just say the affirmation, but truly mean it. See if those weaknesses transform or dissipate. Know that where the mind goes is what creates your reality. If there is something you are healing from, notice that when you stop talking about it, it is no longer in your awareness and it is also no longer an issue to heal. I knew I was not healed in regards to all matters surrounding my divorce until it was no longer coming up in conversation. It comes up far less often than it once did, so I know that all my traumas and dramas around it are transforming into a healthier place. What are you talking about that is creating or shifting your reality? What can you do to shift this reality? Can you be thankful for the awareness, create a positive affirmation, and shift out of your mind and into a powerful new awareness of a new glorious life of your very own creation? What does this new visualization look like? Can you see yourself empowered?

Tips For Stepping Into Your Becoming

1. Keep a dream journal. Find common themes in waking and sleeping states.
2. Be conscious of what you are creating in your life. Then go create it.
3. Create a list of positive affirmations for each area you wish to shift; then believe in those affirmations and see the situation shifting.

EXERCISE:

Begin dreaming of the best possible life for yourself and others around you. Get crazy and dream big. Turn your "it will never happen's" into new possibilities. What miracles can you make happen with your thoughts and shifted awareness? Make notes here: ______

When you get out of bed each morning, ask yourself, "What do I want my reality to look like today?" Shift from the want to the having. Remember, you get more reason for wanting by wanting. See it as already so.

Today I am creating: ____________________

Today I am manifesting: ____________________

Today I am feeling: ____________________

Today I am successful at: ____________________

AWAKEN — TRANSFORM — REALIZE

Chapter 9

Learning to Be You

"You change the world by being yourself."

— Yoko Ono

The conflict between I and thou is always reflective. The mind is always a separate identity. If you can conquer your mind's negativity, your bad thoughts, and your lowest self, you can, as Yogi Bhajan said, "Win the whole world." The mind is an identity that needs to be controlled. For example, when you don't have wealth, you are upset and want it, but when you have it, you are worried someone will come and take it away. Your fear is always a guiding factor. When you feel fear or feel insecure, at that moment, you have disconnected from the creator. Be led by God, be committed to self. Trust that the power that created you will take care of you. Self-negativity magnifies the need for apathy. Many people need apathy because they have no self-respect. You don't need help if you channel into the divine within you and worship the identity God gave you.

The most precious thing is not what people say about you, but what you say to and about yourself. People act as your actions say. If you cannot uplift yourself with your own self, you have to correct your being. Every sentence spoken has an effect on you. Can you talk to your own consciousness and be clear? God made you to learn…to learn to be you—by reverence, grace, selflessness, and self-esteem.

Yogi Bhajan often asked: "Are you looking at your own soul (or looking for a soulmate)?" Is your soul your companion? Are you identifying with your own identity? What is the truth of your identity? Learn to be you, and learn to be whom God made you to be. If your presence cannot have radiance, you cannot guide yourself, and if you cannot be yourself, there is something wrong and you have not accepted the divine within and around you. The main contribution to your own self-destruction is denial of the divine within.

Have faith in the creator. Yogi Bhajan said, "Excuses are self-abuses." In the end, you have dug your own ditch, and no one is responsible for you but you. He stated that the Sikh philosophy was always to let your relationship with yourself be better than it was yesterday. If you are not learning to do self-therapy, you are not learning. You need to talk to your own soul, not a therapist. Man is intoxicated and blind in his ego. Once you start learning on your own path, you know how to walk. Once the shabd (voice or song) of the guru (the bringer of light from the dark) comes into your heart, you know how to talk. Once you identify yourself, you know how to be. Walk this path with the strength of self.

Tips for Stepping Into You:

1. Meditate to find the divine within you.

2. Express your uniqueness daily.
3. Spend some time alone.
4. Make a list of what you value.
5. Connect to your childhood passions.
6. Create something—draw, paint, build, or write.
7. Find your mantra.
8. Have faith in your creator.
9. Have a therapy session with Self.
10. Make a list of your must-have soulmate qualities and see how those are reflected in your Self. What do you need from *you* rather than a soulmate?

Mastering Your Desires

"For the rational, healthy person, the desire for pleasure
is the desire to celebrate his control over reality.
For the neurotic, the desire for pleasure
is the desire to escape from reality."

— Nathaniel Branden

The energy behind desire is essential to life. Desires can be healthy and motivating but they can also move into unhealthy addictions. Without healthy desires, we would have no forward movement within ourselves or our world. We have a natural urge to take action and create. We are all born with desires. But how do we burn through ego and master desires to steer our lives?

Once you bring full awareness into the mind, everything changes. With awareness, you can even step back from any addiction to follow desire, and then a doorway magically opens to a very spiritual experience of life. You don't get hooked or sidetracked by another desire because you realize they are all going to manifest one day at the right time. You don't walk into any situation that doesn't enhance your grace.

Once you find your tool(s) and/or practice(s) that helps move you into your feel good place, then you can begin to master the manifestation of your desires. Finding that tool starts with commitment and defining a goal. Focus on attracting the feel good things first and then you will find your way to attracting the material "stuff" later. When you feel good, you energetically attract more goodness. One tool might simply be surrounding yourself with people and places that help you feel good and more aligned with your goals. Surround yourself with people, places, and things that enhance your grace.

This is personally one of my greatest struggles, as I tend to notice I have compassion for people who are or who have struggled deeply at various stages of their lives. I get buried in their struggles and try to help instead of focusing on the feel good stuff that is more aligned with my goals and desires. I've learned we tend to have compassion for that which we understand or have experienced. Therefore, I went through a spell of attracting people who are shifting through huge transformational periods in their lives. When this happened, I began to become overwhelmed with how I could help them. It drained me. It doesn't always bring me joy to help and I end up helping out of guilt instead of love. It messes with my grace.

Whatever life throws at you, you must respond from a place of love to be sure there is a vibrational match at the level of love, not guilt. It is my desire to help, but then I realize sometimes the best help is none at all. The best help you can sometimes give is holding the space, walking away, and letting them shift through those transformational periods on their own so that they can find their strength and you can continue to focus on what brings you happiness, joy, and growth for your highest good.

Honoring yourself is by no means selfish. You are only as good to/for others as you are to/for yourself. I've caught myself asking: "Is it appropriate to walk away from someone who claims to need your help when you know you can help them but just don't want to for whatever reason?" Sometimes walking away is all the help they need for self-empowerment and healing. Every relationship is based on each person's emotional security. When we need to let someone or something go, we must also do this with grace. If it does not serve your grace, let it go, but do not let your grace fall apart. When we see what it is that we don't want, we can better see that which we do want. Occasionally, it takes seeing someone else suffering to identify further those pieces of self that are suffering. By stepping away to reflect on the mirror, you are helping yourself and helping the other person who gifted you with that reflection for self-care. Helping you *is* helping others! Be there for another only when you can do so while standing fully in happiness.

Happiness is ultimately our true manifestation. We must step out of the reflections of self that challenge or dim the light of our desires or grace and pull us into a downward spiral of unhappiness and disbelief of the power of self. We must learn ways to enhance our happiness and empower all the facets of reality that fulfill our desires and allow us to stand in grace. We must maintain a vibration to match to our desires and happiness, not our fears and disbeliefs. Happiness is your birthright.

Release all the disbelief in your power to be happy. Simply praying for the release of your fears is a great place to start. Ask God to set you free from all the limiting beliefs that block you from your greatness. Stay open to signs from God, and be present with everything that presents itself (even if it temporarily brings discomfort). Doing sit-ups or running a mile isn't always easy, but the results far outweigh the temporary discomfort; being open to the good coming to you is no different; make space in your being for the more positive experiences you will attract into your life.

You must be clear about what you want to bring into your life. Otherwise, you may attract what you don't want, although that will also teach you more about what you do want. A great way to get clear is to create a list or a vision board to identify what you want. Don't worry about how odd or unconventional anything you include might seem. Again, try to focus on the feel good items instead of the material "stuff." Do whatever is needed to get the mental picture of your desires. Clarify how you want to feel, and begin to access that feeling.

Spend time every day sitting in the feeling of what you desire. Use meditation or any other visioning exercise that works for you. Call on this feeling while doing menial tasks or driving in your car. Let the feeling, not the wanting, take over your being. The more you feel the feeling, the more you believe what you want is on its way to you. If you truly believe it is already here, then it will be. And you might be surprised by what form it shows up in. When you are certain it will show up, you can sit back, relax, and allow. God generally has a much better plan for how this will unfold than you can imagine. God has your back, so push your disbelief aside and simply allow. Accept your greatness. You are already living in your greatness. Regardless of what is happening outside, the good stuff is going on inside. Trust that you are given everything that you need when you need it.

See the power inside you. Know that whatever you want in life wants you. One day it is going to manifest, whether it happens in this lifetime or the next. The next lifetime may only be a blink away in the infinite time and space of your soul's existence. Relax, breathe deeply, and feel the infinite being you truly are. Begin to see your desires as a fun and enlightening experience meant to awaken your soul to the vastness of your being. Then you will start to enjoy your journey through life so much more because your happiness is not dependent upon what does or doesn't manifest. God has your back, and everything you desire will come to you when the timing is right.

Ending Your Suffering

"The mind craves for formulations and definitions,
always eager to squeeze reality into a verbal shape.
A quiet mind is all you need.
All else will happen rightly, once your mind is quiet."

— *Nisargadatta Maharaj*

A secret to mastering desire is knowing that your level of suffering solely depends on how attached you are to a certain desire. *If you have no attachment, there is no suffering.* This wisdom is one of the greatest tools you can use on the path toward enlightenment. Take notice of what gets under your skin. Did you find the perfect house, but then you had to wait to hear from the sellers and the bank. Are you planning how perfect your life is going to be once you move there and feeling frustrated that it isn't happening as quickly as you want? Maybe God has another plan that's greater than your own? Maybe a different house or different timing will ultimately work better for you, though you can't see it now? Maybe you will suddenly discover you have a different job in a different state where your real dream home is waiting for you. Maybe an inheritance comes and you buy an even better home....

The more aware you become that your level of attachment is creating all of your suffering, the greater chance you have for mastery over your life. When you realize you are an all-powerful, infinite being who can manifest anything by pure will, you won't be attached to anything anymore. Life is an endless journey. By discovering the suffering we incur is a clue to understanding our patterns, we take a step toward truly becoming free. A wise master exists inside you who sees the pain caused by your attachment to desire. This divine self inside of you can liberate you and keep a watch over your mind's busyness. When you feel suffering, practice noticing which desire you are attached to. Choose to remain conscious and you'll soon free yourself from the pain by relinquishing your attachment to your desires.

A magical manifesting power exists within you that will bring any desire into manifestation effortlessly. Your manifestation has already happened. Surrender the mind. The Universe also accepts that what you desire is your truth, so it brings that desire into absolute reality. When you can live your life fully from this conscious place, you can make any wish you want manifest in your life. God hears your every desire as a command and simply manifests it for you at the perfect time and place. Energy flows where energy (or thought) goes.

Imagine what your life will be like when you are free from attachment to all your desires. Explore the part of you that is already free. When you start believing the power of your thoughts without expectation, the Universe responds accordingly! The Universe must follow your beliefs because what you believe is like a command to the creation. The more convinced you are that something is true, the quicker the Universe supports you in making it manifest.

"Imagination is the greatest creative force in the Universe."

— Albert Einstein

Tips for Stepping Into Your Becoming:

1. Say nice things about yourself.
2. See the divine within you.
3. Release your attachment to end your suffering.
4. Your manifestation has already happened. Believe it.
5. Give something away that you feel really attached to.

EXERCISE:

Practice positive affirmations, but don't just say them. Believe them. List them here. ______________________________

____

____

____

____

____

____

What are you so attached to that you think you can't live without it? Practice living without it until you release your attachment. How does it feel to release it?

What do you want to manifest into your life? Do you believe you can? Define it here; then practice living like you already have it. (Then, just for fun, do it again.)

AWAKEN — TRANSFORM — REALIZE

Chapter 10

The Power of Belief

"You can have anything you want
if you will give up the belief that you can't have it."

— Dr. Robert Anthony

Having Faith

Belief is a bit like having faith, but it's also a sense of knowing your belief will manifest with the helping hand of faith. Faith involves a level of surrender. Whatever faith you have inside you will determine the outcome. If you don't have belief or faith, then you won't expect anything to manifest. Faith helps us overcome our fear of pain, grief, and disappointment, and stay open to new experience and understanding. In a way, faith is a bit like being open to what scares us. What you spend your money, time, and energy on will show you in return how much faith or belief you have put into the divine. What manifests in your life is a good indication of your beliefs. If you are struggling, then perhaps it's karma, or perhaps you don't believe life can be different, better? Or perhaps you don't have faith that it can or will? If you read the Christian gospels, you will see how much Jesus loved and always responded to anyone who had faith. Because of my love for dogs I love this story:

> Then Jesus left Galilee and went north to the region of Tyre and Sidon. A Gentile woman who lived there came to him, pleading, "Have mercy on me, O Lord, Son of David! For my daughter is possessed by a demon that torments her severely." But Jesus gave her no reply, not even a word. Then his disciples urged him to send her away. "Tell her to go away," they said. "She is bothering us with all her begging." Then Jesus said to the woman, "I was sent only to help God's lost sheep—the people of Israel." But she came and worshiped him, pleading again, "Lord, help me!" Jesus responded, "It isn't right to take food from the children and throw it to the dogs." She replied, "That's true, Lord, but even dogs are allowed to eat the scraps that fall beneath their masters' table." "Dear woman," Jesus said to her, "your faith is great. Your request is granted." And her daughter was instantly healed. (Matthew 15:21-28)

It was faith that made what this woman desired manifest despite the obstacles in her way—that she was a Gentile, not a Jew. She refused to let those obstacles overcome her faith. You've probably also heard that Jesus said: "I tell you the truth, if you had faith even as small as a mustard seed, you could say to this mountain, 'Move from here to there,' and it would move. Nothing would be impossible." Jesus compared our faith to a mustard seed, and a seed is worth more when it continues to grow. If you water and feed it, it grows. Similarly, you must feed your faith with positive thoughts. The Bible states that faith comes from God and it is a gift. You do not need to earn a gift.

Instead, it is just given to you. So whatever you desire is available to you. You just have to ask and believe it will be given; then it is yours. If we have trouble believing what we need will be given, we can begin by asking God for more faith so we will believe what God says to us is true, even if we don't see it happen right away.

"So I say to you, ask, and it will be given to you;
seek, and you will find; knock, and it will be opened to you.
For everyone who asks, receives; and he who seeks, finds;
and to him who knocks, it will be opened…."

— Luke 11: 9-10

I experienced a powerful lesson in faith when the time came for us to move to Hawaii. When I first got my three new puppies, I knew Shiitake had taught me many lessons about diet and health care I would use in both my life and the lives of these new pups. I knew it was very likely she became ill because of the double dose of mandatory rabies shots she had to have prior to coming to Maui. Maui is a rabies free island, so she and Sushi had to go through many months of quarantine prior to traveling there. I cringed both times they had to have their shots, but I took a chance or leap of faith, believing the vets knew what they were doing and she would be fine. I know now that no matter what choice I made, her plans for departure were imminent, but it's hard to be okay with that when such a young animal becomes ill. I knew I didn't want to have to worry about the reactions the new pups might have to such things so I decided to research immunizations. After many months of lost sleep and reading countless studies of more cons than pros, I decided that going forward, I was going to trust in God. God created these little beings, so I decided I would not alter that perfection with immunizations, but instead have faith that they were built strong and their lives were purposeful.

I thought back when my ex-husband and I had our chiropractic offices. One client decided to use chiropractic as her primary form of pregnancy care. She told us how she was also going to have a home birth. We really didn't pay much attention to her choices—until one day she carried in her newborn son. She told us how she had sent her husband and two boys to their cabin for the weekend; then she proceeded to fill up her birthing tub with warm water and prepare to give birth in the "peace and care of the Lord." We had always thought her a bit strange, but now, as I sat with my pups, I realized she was a woman of faith. She put her and her child's care in God's hands. She told us about the whole process and how when her husband and boys came home she introduced them to the new baby. It took me years of reflection to understand that she was not crazy, but just very trusting in the power that created her.

Remembering her made me realize that if I chose not to immunize, I was not doing anything wrong, but I was trusting in God, trusting in nature, trusting in the strength of these little beings and their willingness to live. For the first six months I was worried about taking them out of the house, but I read that many people actually suggest taking unimmunized pets to places where the disease and bacteria they would be immunized against actually lived so they could be exposed to them and build up an immunity. This would teach their little bodies how to combat things like parvo and distemper. It made sense to me. I was nervous, but I trusted. The research I was reading indicated that even if they did come in contact with parvo their chances of survival were greater if they never had the immunizations to begin with. I was shocked by that, but I read that everywhere I looked. And I learned as well that distemper is not really even something that dogs are very likely to come into contact with these days. I was beginning to see how I had been programmed into certain beliefs, and I wasn't even sure why I gave all my other animals immunizations. I did it only because I was told to. I even learned that to give a puppy any immunization prior to twelve weeks was pointless anyhow because they still have their mother's antibodies.

I thought that I had broken out of "the system," but this period in my life had me realizing that I wasn't always asking questions as to why certain things in my life were done. I realized that if I simply handed things over to the veterinarian, I would be filling my pups with toxins. The veterinarians were making big money on immunizations and many hadn't even researched alternatives. Instead, I handed things over to God and asked myself, "If God created me, why would I be created to be anything other than greatness?" We are all created with the powerful force of all that is, which allows us to stand powerfully in who and what we are. If God is infinite and all powerful then God couldn't do any better if He tried. I found that talking and praying to God during this time was like being held in the arms of a divine mother. We would all be okay. I was not wrong in my choices. There was no wrong. There just was me, the pups, and God.

The pups are now eighteen months old, and, as it would turn out, Bella developed an autoimmune deficiency at one point; had she been given the immunizations, it might have likely killed her body's immune system, depriving her of the strength to survive. Instead of the immunizations, I supplemented with herbs and vitamins to increase the pups' immune systems. I have not needed to step foot in the veterinarian's office for anything. We actually don't even do flea or tick meds anymore because we found out that by having strong immune systems, the fleas and ticks are no longer attracted to them.

Our bulldog is the only hiking bulldog we know of, and she goes on countless hikes with us that are several miles long three or four times per week. Our Shar Pei sprint, run, and jump with several ounces of water in their backpacks on those same hikes. Their teeth are whiter than those of most dogs we know; their eyes are brighter, and overall, they are vibrant. The breeders have even begun to ask me what I'm doing. A combination of no immunizations, a healthy diet, and exercise have worked wonders for these pups. The whole experience has taught me to have faith in my beliefs and in God. Life is purposeful, and the Creator is looking out for His own. We are blessed.

Praying from the Soul

Yogi Bhajan said: "Normally there is no power in the human but the power of prayer. And to do prayer, you have to put your mind and body together and then pray from the soul. Ardas Bahee is a mantra prayer. If you sing it, your mind, body, and soul automatically combine and without saying what you want, the need of the life is adjusted. That is the beauty of this prayer." The words are as follows:

Ardas Bhaee Amar Das Guru,
Amar Das Guru, Ardas Bhaee,
Ram Das Guru, Ram Das Guru,
Ram Das Guru, Sachee Sahee

Translated they mean:

Guru Amar Das is the energy of grace and hope when there is no hope. Guru Ram Das is the energy of miracles, healings, and blessings.

To explain further...*Guru* is that which directs us from darkness (gu) to light (ru), from ignorance to the experience of our infinite nature. The Ardaas Bahee mantra may be translated, "The prayer that has been made to Guru Amar Das is guaranteed by Guru Ram Das." This is the mantra for answered prayers.

Guru Amar Das is the third of the Sikh Gurus. He lived from 1479 to 1574. He is said to embody generosity and equality. Guru Ram Das, his son-in-law, is the fourth of the Sikh Gurus. He lived from 1534 until 1581. He is said to embody humility, loving service, and compassion. *Ram* means "servant of the Lord." It is said that if you ask something of Guru Ram Das, he has to bring it to God for you. Give your worries to Guru Ram Das and let him take them to God. The God that rotates the earth can certainly take care of your problems! This is the prayer to answer all prayers.

Sharing our beliefs or our faith with others about our goals, dreams, or visions helps make them a reality. If you believe something, it is the most powerful message you can carry because you will become a divine inspiration to others, proving to them that God is listening and helping manifest your reality through the power of your beliefs. When we believe in something, it becomes truth—it becomes magic.

Utilizing Your Power

By utilizing your conscious power to choose your beliefs, you will dramatically enhance the quality of all aspects of your life. It's your belief (or non-belief) in something that determines whether or not you are able to accomplish it. Regardless of the size or scope of the event or circumstance being considered or who you are, where you live, or what your religious preference (or lack thereof) might be, the power of *your* belief is behind it all.

The outcome of your belief is dependent on whether you believe the thing can (or can't) manifest. The power of your belief is what enables and allows miracles to unfold. I have to think karma can even be overridden with commitment because sooner or later God will reward the commitment of character and the power of belief. Sooner or later, God will adjust your karma if you stay committed. Belief far outweighs any karma! There is absolutely nothing the human mind can conceive or imagine that cannot or will not be brought into physical manifestation at some point. Every thought that goes through your mind goes into the Universe to create your reality. You can think something but still not become it if you believe you will fail at it. Beliefs are more powerful than thoughts. You actually have to believe something even more than you feel it. Belief makes a difference. If you don't believe in positive affirmations, then repeating them millions of times will manifest nothing. Belief is the magic that transforms your reality. Saying isn't believing.

Believing is manifesting. If something is troublesome in your life, not as you wish it to be, then you might want to take a much closer and deeper look at your beliefs. Do you want something other than what you have? Stop the wanting and start the believing! Truly believing. You are literally creating your reality with your thoughts, emotions, actions, and beliefs. Touch it, feel it, taste it, and know it!

When we come to this planet, we are closer to Source, but as time goes by and we age, we become subject to rules, conditioning, and the beliefs of those around us. We lose the connection we once had with Source if we aren't living in our faith. We become wounded in many cases. Our beliefs become skewed and limited based on our surroundings. We are told we are not good enough. We are basically molded to forget what we once knew from Source—that we are unlimited. Our potential is vast. We are conditioned to fall into certain social molds. If we don't, we are sometimes labeled with terms like ADD, ADHD, and other behavior disorders. Then we are forced to be something we are not. We become self-limiting, and it's not generally our fault. We are just conditioned. One example that always saddens me is when someone becomes sick or is just socially inept in some way and it's blamed on someone else—"Well, that just runs in our family."

By allowing ourselves to be convinced someone else is stronger, more knowledgeable, more moral, closer to God, or just more powerful (whatever that means) than we are, we have in effect participated in our own enslavement. The only thing that can keep a belief from manifesting in physical form is a shift in the belief or faith of the person who originally conceived the thought. Doubt (non-belief) is established through the same process. Doubt begins as a thought, which also stems from a belief that ignites and creates an emotion (fear-based), which creates the physical manifestation of the absence of the thing thought of. Or doubt creates more of what you fear and don't want! Be careful what you believe because it's true. Be careful what you doubt because that is true, too!

"Doubt is the father of invention."

— Ambrose Bierce

Wrestling with Doubt

Doubt is central to belief; even believers have it. You don't have to be religious to have it. But we can see doubt as a gift because when our desire is answered, our faith grows stronger and teaches us not to doubt. No matter how strong our faith is, at some point, we experience doubt or inner conflict. Instead of being a sign of weakness, doubt can actually be something that causes us to dig deeper into our relationship with self or the divine and can even make our faith stronger. Conflicts come to test your faith. Doubt and faith speak no particular religious language. They are universal. Here are words spoken by masters about faith and doubt at points where they have been challenged in their lives:

"Faith, in the sense in which I am here using the word,
is the art of holding on to things your reason has once accepted,
in spite of your changing moods ...
That is why Faith is such a necessary virtue:
unless you teach your moods 'where they get off,'
you can never be either a sound Christian or even a sound atheist."

— C.S. Lewis

"Darkness is such that I really do not see—
neither with my mind nor with my reason—
the place of God in my soul is blank—
There is no God in me—
when the pain of longing is so great—
I just long & long for God....
The torture and pain I can't explain."

— Mother Teresa

"For more than a week I was close to the gates of death and hell.
I trembled in all my members.
Christ was wholly lost.
I was shaken by desperation and blasphemy of God.'"

— Martin Luther King, Jr.

C.S. Lewis struggled with the intellectual side of faith. Mother Theresa frequently prayed for God to heal her loneliness and feelings of isolation from God, yet her devotion to her calling never wavered. Martin Luther King, Jr. suffered a period of depression and doubted his own character.

In Buddhist practices, doubt is part of a text from the Pali Canon called *The Five Mental Hindrances and Their Conquest.* Doubt sits among other "hindrances" such as sensual desire, ill-will, sloth, torpor, restlessness, and remorse. Some forms of Buddhism say doubt is generally considered a kind of poison and encourage faith. However, Zen Buddhism has a practice intended to arouse doubt because it is believed that with great doubt, great awakening exists, and with little or no doubt, you guessed it—there is little or no awakening. It is believed that with Great Doubt, Great Trust arises. Great Trust is the conviction that there is a way. Great Doubt provides the fuel to go all the way: "Fully trust, you'll fully doubt; fully doubt, you'll fully awaken." Whatever you encounter, there can be no doubt or no hesitation. However, a kind of trust is needed because doubt cannot be avoided. The self is split with faith and with doubt.

In Zen practice, it is said that doubt falls into a kind of mental scattering, and if trust is firm, doubt will be firm and the mental scattering will naturally vanish. Doubt and faith, more or less, coexist with one another. Having this mental scattering resolved once and for all is at the heart of Zen Buddhism. "Faith" might be defined as an absence of doubt, and "doubt" as an absence of faith. A Zen student is encouraged to cultivate both.

Faith and doubt are supposed to be opposites, but if we have no faith, we have no doubt. True faith requires true doubt; without doubt, faith is not faith. This kind of faith is not the same thing as certainty, and it's not about denial and disbelief; it is more like trust, openness, and living in an open-hearted and courageous way. (It is called "shraddha" in the Buddhist teachings.) Pema Chodron said, "We can let the circumstances of our lives harden us so that we become increasingly resentful and afraid, or we can let them soften us and make us kinder and more open to what scares us. We always have this choice."

"At the bottom of Great Doubt lies Great Awakening.
If you doubt fully you will awaken fully."

— Master Hakuin

To achieve enlightenment, sitting in meditation with self can be helpful. The "Loving-Kindness Meditation" is very popular in the Buddhist tradition for this purpose. The goal is to break through self and go to where self is gone. It is said you cannot sit and wait for something to happen—"awaiting-enlightenment"—because if you do, then you are not giving yourself fully to the practice. Just be open and doubt will immediately arise; when you reach your limit, you'll naturally awaken.

One of the many things I like about Buddhism is its acknowledgment that none of its theories, ideologies, or practices are absolute truth, but are meant to give guidance on your spiritual journey.It really is a form of "practice." "Take one leap after another in the darkness until the light shines," is a Zen saying.

"When you doubt your power,
you give power to your doubt."

— Honore de Balzac

EXERCISE:

METTA MEDITATION (Loving-Kindness Meditation)

The Loving-Kindness Meditation focuses on developing feelings of goodwill, kindness, and warmth toward others. Reciting specific words and phrases evokes a "boundless warmhearted feeling." The Metta meditation is regularly recommended to the Buddha's followers in the Pali canon. The canon advises spreading metta to whatever beings there may be. There are successive stages of meditation during which one progressively cultivates kindness toward oneself, a good friend, a "neutral" person, a difficult person, all four of the above equally, and then gradually the entire universe. The strength of this feeling is not limited to or by family, religion, or social class. The following is a basic set of instructions for the practice from the book *The Issue at Hand* by Gil Fronsdal.

Instructions for Loving-Kindness Meditation*

To practice loving-kindness meditation, sit in a comfortable and relaxed manner. Take two or three deep breaths with slow, long, and complete exhalations. Let go of any concerns or preoccupations. For a few minutes, feel or imagine the breath moving through the center of your chest—in the area of your heart.

Metta is first practiced toward oneself, since we often have difficulty loving others without first loving ourselves. Sitting quietly, mentally repeat, slowly and steadily, the following or similar phrases:

May I be happy.
May I be well.
May I be safe.
May I be peaceful and at ease.

While you say these phrases, allow yourself to sink into the intentions they express. Loving-kindness meditation consists primarily of connecting to the intention of wishing ourselves or others happiness. However, if feelings of warmth, friendliness, or love arise in the body or mind, connect to them, allowing them to grow as you repeat the phrases. As an aid to the meditation, you might hold an image of yourself in your mind's eye. This helps reinforce the intentions expressed in the phrases.

After a period of directing loving-kindness toward yourself, bring to mind a friend or someone in your life who has deeply cared for you.

---

* *http://www.mettainstitute.org/mettameditation.html*

Then slowly repeat phrases of loving-kindness toward them:

May you be happy.
May you be well.
May you be safe.
May you be peaceful and at ease.

As you say these phrases, again sink into their intention or heartfelt meaning. And, if any feelings of loving-kindness arise, connect the feelings with the phrases so that the feelings may become stronger as you repeat the words.

As you continue the meditation, you can bring to mind other friends, neighbors, acquaintances, strangers, animals, and finally people with whom you have difficulty. You can either use the same phrases, repeating them again and again, or make up phrases that better represent the loving-kindness you feel toward these beings. In addition to simple and perhaps personal and creative forms of metta practice, there is a classic and systematic approach to metta as an intensive meditation practice. Because the classic meditation is fairly elaborate, it is usually undertaken during periods of intensive metta practice on retreat.

Sometimes during loving-kindness meditation, seemingly opposite feelings such as anger, grief, or sadness may arise. Take these to be signs that your heart is softening, revealing what is held there. You can either shift to mindfulness practice or you can—with whatever patience, acceptance, and kindness you can muster for such feelings—direct loving-kindness toward them. Above all, remember that there is no need to judge yourself for having these feelings.

This meditation is growing in popularity and is said to help with the following: well-being, healing, emotional intelligence, stress, social connections, and self-love.

Polarity of Lack

Thoughts make up your reality because thoughts turn into beliefs. Once you have a belief, you have a little ball of manifesting energy that becomes physical. Imagine if you changed your thoughts from limited and finite to unlimited and infinite. You exist in an infinite universe that is more than capable of bringing you whatever you can conceive and believe it can. You must start focusing on what you consciously and subconsciously want, not on what you don't. (Conflicting beliefs keep your manifestations from being realized.) But wants are different than beliefs. Here's where it gets interesting... simply the fact that you want something, whatever it is, could be a factor in keeping it from manifesting in your life.

At a subconscious or spiritual level, there is no such thing as polarity. Polarity is a physical thing. First of all, the fact that you want something implies lack. Did you catch that? *The fact that you want something implies lack.* Wanting a thing means that you don't have it. That wanting creates a specific emotion within you that emanates energy or a vibration of "I don't have." The universe hears "I want it. I don't have it." So the universe gives you more of the state of "want" or "not having." You must shift the "want" to an inner knowing that you already have. After you shift your beliefs, you must align the belief with what is desired. You must believe it is your birthright to have it; become aware of your ability to attract it; put your thoughts and emotions in alignment with its manifestation through some form of visualization exercise; be thankful you have already received it; detach yourself from the when and how; expect whatever it is will arrive.

About a year ago, I had a moment of awakening in my yoga practice. I met with a teacher to discuss a plan for my spiritual and yoga practice. I wanted to dedicate myself to my daily practice more than I had been. I asked how I could connect deeper to the voice of the infinite. I essentially wanted to know how to talk to God better. I wanted to develop a pipeline to God. I viewed this as an infinite etheric place. This place was outside of me where possibilities and answers to my questions were unlimited, bountiful, infinite. I realized what I was basically saying was I wanted to connect with something greater than myself that was present in a non-earthly place.

My teacher tuned into that pipeline, giving me my lesson plan. I watched as the information telepathically streamed in. His eyes fluttered, and I jealously sat watching the download take place. I wanted that connection too. I wondered whether I was honestly doing the work to develop that pipeline, but I also watched how access to that information came into the physical and became a part of both of our realities.

As the information was being shared with me, I understood exactly what this practice was going to do for me. It was a language that spoke to me as my teacher waved his hands, motioning me to sit a certain way and place my hands in a certain mudra (hand position). I read exactly what it was going to do for me. It was basically going to cut through the red tape of the infinite and the finite, the earthly and the divine. Without practicing it for months on end, I could see its effects and purpose immediately as he was explaining it to me.

I mention this experience because it was given to me to shift my belief system. It was given to me so I could see there truly is no division between the physical and some imaginary place that didn't exist on earth. I saw the infinite was right there for me to reach into and, just as Shiitake showed me when she passed, it was all encompassing and within my every fiber. I just had to stop intentionally and unintentionally blocking it.

It was scary for me to think there didn't need to be a barrier between what is often thought of as the knowing and the unknowing or the physical and ethereal. Limiting beliefs, fear, and social conditioning were my barriers to living my life more fully. But the kicker to it all was that I also learned I should not place such importance on something that exists elsewhere. The meditation I was given showed me that it was equally as important to connect to the spiritual as the physical. I was beginning to see that incarnating into the physical was purposeful and intentional, and I had placed so much importance for so many years on connecting to something someplace other than here!

Why do you suppose that nature is provided for with no effort on its part? Perhaps there are no false beliefs or social conditionings that block the birds or flowers from being provided for because it is just their birthright. They don't fear or worry they will go hungry, have no shelter, or lose their jobs. They haven't been taught as we humans have. They receive effortlessly and continually because they believe no differently. We are small little beings in this ecosystem on earth and in the universe; we'd have to be pretty naive to believe we are all alone, or that the power that created us is not going to take care of us. Just stop and think about that for a moment. Something larger than us created us for a purpose. We are purposeful beings! If you had the power to create life, wouldn't you watch and care for it? If you've ever given birth to another human, a thought, a project, or cared for a child, puppy, or kitten, you know you love it deeply so you watch over its wellbeing. Isn't this what happens for us with God? Nature (plants and animals) teach us we need to stop worrying so we can more effectively and effortlessly create, attract, and experience our most desired dreams and visions.

Unlearning False Beliefs

We need to step away from the outcome and unlearn many of our false beliefs. They keep us stuck in a world full of limitation. We need to break free from this cycle and teach our children the importance of nature, compassion, dreaming a positive world into being, and our limitless potential, instead of teaching the importance of owning more material possessions or competing with our neighbors. We have become a materialistic world, and the distractions of such a world keep us from finding ourselves and our personal power. We are kept in a mind-numbing state instead of being educated and trained to live to our fullest potential. It's a sad state when yoga, natural health, and spiritual studies are ridiculed or called "alternative." People with such mindsets behave from their own fears of success and wellness. Are we allowing others' fears to become our own without even knowing it? Or are we truly creating our reality?

"Do not believe in anything simply because you have heard it.
Do not believe in anything simply because
it is spoken and rumored by many.
Do not believe in anything simply because
it is found written in your religious books.
Do not believe in anything merely on
the authority of your teachers and elders.

Do not believe in traditions because they
have been handed down for many generations.
But after observation and analysis,
when you find that anything agrees with reason and
is conducive to the good and benefit of one and all,
then accept it and live up to it."

— Buddha

Many great techniques and technologies are out there for breaking up and unlearning limiting beliefs, such as maybe Theta Healing or Emotional Freedom Technique? Quantum Physics is starting to prove *you* are responsible for *whatever* outcomes you are experiencing in your life. A power created us and cares about our wellbeing, and that same power allows us the ability to figure out solutions on our own because doing so truly gives us our own strength. Have you ever been sick, but once you felt better, you felt better than ever and were prepared to take on the world?

The down times we have in life prepare us for the go times. When we are slowed down, we have time to connect and time to think. We begin to appreciate our health. We begin to appreciate those around us who care for and love us. We are thankful for moments of love and comfort. When we are sad and depressed, those who stick with us prove their friendship. And it's normal as we move from that sadness and depression that those friends who were there with us move away, too, because they were attracted to us in a lower vibration. If they truly move through with us, they heal alongside of us.

The best gift we can give back to all those around us is patience. We are all here on earth to learn and grow; that is truly our purpose here. If we simply view each other as students of life, then we cannot (or will not) fault each other for the process and rate at which we learn. It can be especially important to see family members as students and teachers. We chose them before incarnating so we could learn from those always close to us. Practice forgiveness and release expectations that family members are supposed to "serve" you in a different way than complete strangers. Say this to each person you have challenges with right now: "I have no expectations from or of you, and I forgive all occurrences with you that I judge as negative or incomplete. I have compassion for you on this life's journey."

Our power isn't in manipulating others, but in having compassion and guiding and serving those around us. My dad always used to tell me how he wanted a new pair of shoes until one day he met a man with no feet. Our power is within. Our power is the strongest when we get ourselves straightened out and start assisting those who need help more than we do.

"There is no man living that cannot
do more than he thinks he can."

— Henry Ford

Ultimately, the power of belief is that you have a choice as to what you believe, and you have the individual power to choose what works best for you. No matter what situation you find yourself in in your life, there is not one person who owns your beliefs. Your beliefs are unique to you. You own them. You can't say that about many things in your life. Institution, family, and religion might give you guidelines, but, ultimately, you choose what you bring into your reality. Nothing should be accepted on blind faith, but putting aside all assumptions about the nature of self, reality, and existence is a great place to start.

Tips for Stepping Into Your Becoming:

1. Have faith.
2. Pray from your soul.
3. Find your power and be unwavering in your potential.
4. Doubt is not weakness—cherish it and blossom.
5. Step away from wanting and into having or being.
6. Trust in yourself and your intuition.
7. Heal your Self. Then help others awaken, transform, and realize.

EXERCISE:

Have you lost faith? How was it lost, and how could it be restored? Where in your life could you surrender? ______________________

____

____

____

When has faith or doubt caused you to have a deeper connection or belief in the divine? Where has either made you a stronger person?

____

____

____

____

Shift your "wants" into positive "haves"...what do you already have? What are you being already? (Shift "I want a new car" into "Now I have a new car.") ______________________________

____

____

____

____

____

If you were healed and in a perfect state, would you respond to life differently? What would you do if you no longer had perceived wounds? ______________________________

____

____

____

____

____

Practice releasing expectations of those closest to you. Shift your beliefs about how they are supposed to serve you. Begin to ask how you can serve them. Show compassion. Imagine them as butterflies in the palms of your hands, and watch them fly freely away. Make notes here: ______________________________

____

____

____

____

____

AWAKEN — TRANSFORM — REALIZE

Chapter 11

Principles to Live By

"I have only two rules
which I regard as principles of conduct.
The first is: Have no rules.
The second is: Be independent of the opinion of others."

— Albert Einstein

Life is hard. It doesn't matter whether you're living in a mansion or standing in line at a soup kitchen, the truth is not many of us were given the tools or life principles to cope with the many stressors in our lives. If you don't have access to technologies, methodologies, philosophies, life or spiritual practices, or beliefs, you could spend a lifetime trying to educate yourself (or just give up all together). It's one thing to talk about great ideas to "fix" what's not working; it's another to take the time to apply the principles. It's real work. In the chaos of your life, you might think you don't have time, but the reality is if you want to have a better life, you must make the time to change and restructure what's not working. You might be able to put a Band-Aid on a wound, but sooner or later, you need to figure out a solution beyond a temporary cover. We can talk about solutions or we can practice them. I find that involving the body, mind, and spirit in the solution shakes out our bad habits and opens us up to new solutions and ways of living. Whether you choose a sport, a spiritual practice, yoga, a walk in nature, or find a new healing modality or support group, one thing is clear—if you approach it consciously, you can change your life for the better.

Self-Sourcing

You must either find a way to be self-sourcing or become part of something that teaches strong principles to live by. In my case, I learned yoga and shamanism, and they have become the backbone to my existence. But when the training wheels came off, I began to ride on my own without limits imposed by any institution, ritual, or practice. You may have a particular faith that guides and leads you. If you have nothing to lead you, then how can you be led? God can lead; a Guru can lead. But where do they get their information to lead you?

It's great to have a mentor, but you can only go as far as that mentor can, or is willing to, take you. If you reach into infinity, then infinity can send back a wealth of answers that go beyond the limitations of another human. Finding a path to guide or steer you when you need it can also be a lot of fun. It can provide you a friend (in spirit or physically) to talk to when you are out beating the pavement of life. You don't have to go it alone.

It's been said that self-sourcing happens when you let go of reacting.

Meditation is known to be the tool opening you to the messages of the infinite. When you surrender your self-image and stop the mind chatter, you move out of a defensive, reactionary fear mode and let go of resistance; that is where awareness is created. Here all possibilities are open and you can move into Self as Source. Trusting in your joy and not using defensive reasoning allows you to step into a silent, deep relaxing place. The absence of reaction is an active expression of love. Love will teach you once you let go of the ego and self-limiting beliefs. When you stop reacting defensively, your false identity and self-image is put aside; then you can step into the silent comfort of the divine.

When I began my spiritual journey, I tried to find all the positive reasons for doing it. I wanted gumdrops, lollipops, angels, and a pipeline into miracles. I thought I'd live in a heaven on earth. It seemed like a great way to rationalize taking the journey while leaving behind my ex-husband and all that was once meaningful. It was my ego's way of coping with all the change happening in my life. If answers were at the end of the journey, and I'd be comforted when I got there, it would be worth the ride. But as I got farther away from the life I once knew, I was still no closer to what I envisioned stepping into my becoming would look like. I grew exasperated, tired, depressed, and confused. I wondered whether I had made a mistake, taking a journey I shouldn't have. I wondered whether it was all worth it. I wondered whether I was even a better person at this stage in my life than I was when it all began.

I resisted what was negative and chased the positive. But once I realized that God was within both the positive and negative, I began to practice nonresistance. I no longer needed to justify my actions or position. I stepped out of being a hurt victim and faced my shadow self. I chose to see myself as a hero who conquered my Self. I stepped out of depression and into trust, faith, and guidance from the divine. I am not separate from the Source that created me. I am a part of the whole. When you shift into a belief that you are not separate and not left to figure things out alone, but you are gifted with the opportunity to seek answers and then you do, that is divine! God becomes your father, Goddess your mother. You are the divine. When you step into this higher consciousness, you can create. Instead of seeing is believing, you believe to see. You become the seer who not only sees but creates. It takes courage to surrender the ego, but when you do, you step into grace. In this grace, your highest desires are fulfilled without having to strive for them. You become part of a unity consciousness with the divine. You are not just the mirror of others around you, but you are the reflection of the divine. You are the light of God.

I found that in order for me to stay in this kind of consciousness, I needed some kind of regular reminder, so for years I went to yoga classes, shamanic retreats, miscellaneous healing events, and whatever I could. I began to see that I was not always with the like-minded. I approached a period where I was no longer in my ego, but I also no longer resonated with many spiritual communities. I was finding a kind of personal relationship with the creator. I found that adopting other strategies or approaches simply became confusing because those approaches were simply how others found their way. They were not how I found my way. But there were certainly moments when I felt alone and wanted to connect with like-minded people. I tend to believe that's why churches and other institutions are formed. Unfortunately, what often happens is we go to connect, but we end up distracted by entertainers, donation baskets, the need for appropriate attire, and other things that don't assist our personal relationship with the divine. Don't get me wrong. The divine exists in everything, and there are great ways to use that time to understand the Self better.

It's good to surround yourself with what or whom inspires you, to find something you believe in that motivates or excites you, even if it's a quote or a small saying. Although I would not generally claim myself to be a Christian, my mom recently gave me a bracelet with the Serenity Prayer engraved on it. It reminds me to relax, to know I don't have to know everything. Regardless of your spiritual beliefs, these words can provide you with great comfort:

"God, grant me the Serenity to accept the things I cannot change,
the Courage to change the things I can,
and the Wisdom to know the difference."

There are many ways you can become self-sourcing. My furry children are always a great guide for me to find answers. They show me because they can't tell me. I don't just meditate; I also read the signs and symbols in everything. I ask spirit to work with me, using what I'm most comfortable with. Self-sourcing isn't complicated. Just find tools that work for you. You can use divination cards, numbers, dreams, nature, animals, or the mirrors in the life around you. It's just a matter of being consciously aware, so communication will come to you.

Power in Powerlessness

Understanding you can change any awful thing in your life can help you move forward. You must accept that you have the power. The power is in your mind. But there are some things you cannot change, so you must also learn to accept that you can't manage every situation or person. There is great power in powerlessness. Recognizing and admitting powerlessness takes incredible strength and courage.

That night I left Bella on the cliff, I had to let go and trust. I would have clearly died if I tried to save her. The fact is I was born powerless, and I will grow old and weak and eventually die powerless. I had to hope and pray God would intervene. All the finding of myself was no match for the powerlessness I felt while Bella fought for her life. This was truly at a point in my life that tested my faith. There wasn't anything I could do but hope and pray, and pick up the phone and call for help.

My first book was about finding inner truth and awakening. I saw truth as power. The truth in that situation was admitting that I needed a miracle, and I was scared. Bella's incident also symbolized a kind of defeat in other aspects of my life where I admitted I was powerless. I was beginning to take some stress off of myself because I saw that I wasn't perfect. None of us know everything. That's why there are so many of us! Someone else can be what is needed if you can't be it. That's okay. My heart was still wounded from knowing I was not what my ex-husband needed me to be. I saw I was nowhere near the person he needed me to be when I saw the person he chose to be with.

I was learning that it was okay to be me. Bella helped me let go of my expectations of Self. I began to see that I was not powerless, but God just had another plan for me. I was not aware while I was going through the divorce that I would later end up moving from Michigan to Hawaii. I was not aware I would have a beautiful home, a man who loved me, and three amazing new puppies. When I realized I was powerless that night of Bella's accident, it wiped away all the scenarios up until that moment in which I felt I had failed because I couldn't control everything that happened in my life. I saw that power was emerging from my powerlessness. It is an important part of spiritual transformation to recognize where you are powerless. What situation in your life has left you powerless? Did you panic or rely on a force greater than yourself? How did you get through it?

I can't really ever be truly powerless. I used to think I was alone in my pain and struggle, but by having a committed connection to God I saw that night that it was not my time to be a hero; it was God's time to show me where and how to have faith.

"Out of vulnerabilities will come your strength."

— Sigmund Freud

You Have the Power

I used to think other people who were more outspoken and flamboyant were much better leaders than me. I watched them speak loudly and clearly and wondered whether I could ever do that. I felt I had met many people who were on stage with great messages and some who really had no business being on stage. When I watched those who were less educated or less experienced than me take the stage to speak, lead retreats, or write books, I wondered what the difference was between us. I wondered whether they were just meant to do something I wasn't. I figured it must have just been their karma to be earning more, sharing more, teaching more, and generally having a bigger presence than me. I wondered for many years what the difference was between them and me, and why I wasn't also sharing my experiences and knowledge in a more broad way...*and* earning a decent income doing it.

I was scared to write my first book because I was worried what people would think. I didn't want to take the stage because I didn't feel I had a worthwhile message to share. I'm not generally shy, but I have struggled my whole life thinking I was different, and I lacked the confidence that I had a message people wanted to hear. When I joined yoga communities, I noticed a kind of respect happening as I was talking. People were honestly listening for the first time in my life! I actually had my first captive audience. That didn't happen in my career. I saw that my message just wasn't meant for the corporate world. When I found the right place to share my experiences, it seemed people were interested in hearing what I had to say. That gave me more confidence. I learned I was a soft-spoken person, my voice didn't carry well, and I was just meant to share a more experiential spiritual message in a gentle way. Because I was trying to understand how I could share my message, I did some research.

I came across some research by Adam Grant, a psychologist at Wharton and author of *Give and Take*, on how to relate and the power of powerless communication. He basically said that people who are "powerless" admit their shortcomings and use tentative instead of assertive speech. He said some of the world's most powerful communicators use styles that either make them doormats or superstars. He said it boils down to insight. When people think you're trying to influence them, they put their guard up. But when they feel you're trying to help them, or to muse your way to the right answer, or to be honest about your own imperfections, they open up to you and hear what you have to say. Powerless communicators use sentences like, "This might be a good way to go" instead of, "Do it this way." Among salespeople, powerless communicators bring in 68 percent more revenue than "takers" because they ask more and better questions and listen to the answers. Instead of coming on strong, they find out about the hopes and fears of their prospective buyers. They're motivated not only by making the sale, but by satisfying those needs. Buyers feel the difference.

"In a gentle way,
you can shake the world."

— Mahatma Gandhi

If we want to make a change in the world, we need to step up to our fears and stand in the power we have in a divinely guided Self. There really only is faith and trust in the end. Finding our true self is the real power. Remember there is a power greater than you that has your back. When you learn to live in your truth and move out of fear, embracing who you are regardless of what others say or think, you can start taking back your power. When you are fully in your power, you can help others find their way. When you are in your power, you can become thankful for all the things that got you there, no matter how challenging they once were. From a place of faith and trust, you will see that God doesn't just provide warm fuzzies for you; God gives you opportunities to find your Self, see your truth, and ultimately strengthen your faith (in the divine and in the Self) through challenges you face. When we develop a compassion for ourselves, we are surrounded by compassion from and for others. When you find true compassion, there is no other way because what is mirrored back is what you are. Wouldn't it be nice to live in a world full of compassion?

Maybe we should start becoming grateful for all the little things we take for granted each day and build from there? I'm thankful each night for my warm bed full of healthy puppies and the clean water I wash my face and brush my teeth with. Each day, I'm thankful I woke up to start a new adventure of learning more about myself and the world around me. I'm thankful for my awesome Jeep Wrangler and having a man who loves me. I find things throughout my day to give thanks for. I am thankful for all the relationships I have. Some days, I'm not as thankful for the challenging ones, but when I glean the teachings in them, and I see how I can change myself for the better with the ugly mirror they place in front of me, then I am thankful. When I see others around me who are not as well off as I am in some way, I not only become more thankful for what I have, but I try to find ways to be of service. I try to donate to saving animals or helping the homeless with small donations or clothing and supplies. I am thankful for the ability to live consciously in the balance between admitting powerlessness, and at the same time (and through that process), finding the power to make real, powerful, and lasting change.

EXERCISE

Take a look at the following empowering words or phrases, and identify those you use regularly and those you don't use at all. Circle the ideas you want to start implementing in your life. How would making those shifts and changes in your life affect you and others around you?

Accept Yourself	Honor Your Relation-ships	Live in the Moment	Life is Short—Spend Life With People You Like
Know You Can	Let Go	Honor Your Relationships	Live in the Moment
Find Your Truth	Appreciate That You Live in a World of Abundance	Let Go	Take Action—It's a Necessary Part of Success
Realize That Being Good at What You Do Shows in Your Accomplishments	Be of Service	Appreciate That You Live in a World of Abundance	Laugh Often
Be Grateful	Life is Short—Spend Life With People You Like	Be of Service	Self-Source
Invest in Developing Your Consciousness	Live Consciously	The More You Resist The More it Persists	Learn Something New
Be Courageous	Ask for Help When Needed	You Cannot Force Anything Not Meant to Be	Look Inward to Your Reflection in Others
Because You Can't Control The Future, Be Who You Can Be Within the Now	Be Positive to Attract Positive People	Focus on Your Passions	Teach What You Want to Master
Have No Expec-tations	Be Kind	Do What You Love	Realize That You Have a Choice
Do What Brings You Joy	Be Yourself	When in Doubt, Fol-low Your Intuition	Love Yourself
Let Go of the Ener-gy Vampires	Celebrate How Far You've Come	Failure, Frustration, and Criticism Are Part of Success	See Obstacles As Growth, Not An End State
Embrace Change	Love Happens When You Follow Your Life Path	Relish the Moment	Obstacles Deter People Who Don't Want Their Goals Bad Enough
Habits Make You Who You Are—Make Good Ones	Be Confident	You Can't Change Others, But You Can Change Yourself	Create Opportunities; Don't Wait for Them
Challenge Your Fears	Results Are Based on Actions Taken	Focus on Creation	Let Go of What No Longer Serves

Lead By Example	Increase Your Consciousness	Overcome Fear and Pursue Your Dreams	Actively Create Life, Don't Wait for It
Learn to Forgive	Have Faith	Follow Your Passions	Help and Love Others
Give More Than You Receive	Your Level of Success Is Infinite	Trust Your Instincts	See God in Everyone

We only live once. Having great ideas and not sharing them will not change the world around you. Here are some great parallels I have found with my spiritual or yoga teachings and how they guide me every day. These are fun things that teach me how to live and behave in the selling or representation of myself (or my services). I try to bring these concepts or thoughts into my daily activities so I can remind myself that God is everywhere. If you hold a connection to the divine within, then there is no true separation between "church and state" or "divine and institution." And you can still be a spiritual person in a place that's not generally deemed spiritual. The consciousness of the divine will always reside within you. You can be the god light anywhere. That can't be taken away from you even if it's not always welcomed in every environment. But, to be honest, because my spiritual connection is so true for me I tend to find myself, with the Law of Attraction, in places where my spirituality is welcome. Here are some fun practices to play with nonetheless:

YOGA VIRTUE / PRACTICE	LIFE LESSON
Not everyone is flexible.	Be prepared to bend for someone else.
Everyone comes from a different cultural and spiritual background.	Stay neutral.

Take your shoes off before you enter.	Leave your filth out of your business.
Dedicate your practice.	If you cannot show up for you, show up for those you love.
Yoga is a journey of theory and practice.	Life is a journey of theory and practice. Keep practicing what is challenging to develop a level of expertise.
Yoga involves self-discipline.	Develop self-discipline.
Yoga is based on moral virtues like non-violence, truthfulness, righteousness, wisdom, compassion, and kindness.	Hire a yogi. Bring yoga into the work-place.
Practice simplicity.	Don't complicate communication or presentation.
Define a spiritual goal.	Make your goals inclusive of others you interact with, and let others know your blessing upon them.
Sacrifice the ego.	It is not always about you. How may I serve?
Read daily to cleanse spirit and connect with enlightened masters.	Learn from your mentors to perfect your craft.
Be happy and content. Be satisfied with what you have.	You are meant to represent you. Do you well. You are the only you there is.
Persevere when things get difficult.	You have to show up for your life even if you don't want to. It's not about doing as well as others, but doing your personal best. This is not a practice run.
Don't let self-doubt get in the way of your success.	Simply doing something is not enough. You must do it right and with precision. Focus on the actions that create the highest value and know that you are impeccable (highest standards). The quality of your business is a direct reflection of the quality of your self-view.

Always stay positive.	Stay joyful regardless of the outcome. Every entrepreneur experiences failure, but each step brings you closer to learning critical or business lessons that help your growth. Work to experience elevation. Making a difference and making money are not mutually exclusive. When you live a passionate, balanced life full of positivity and good intentions, you create wealth for yourself, your customers, your employees, and the world.
The 5 Sutras of the Aquarian Age by Yogi Bhajan	
Recognize the other person is you.	We are all a part of the same "thing." Learn to treat others not only as you wish to be treated yourself, but ask what you have to offer to help others.
There is a way through every block.	Locate your heart and open your perception to recognize the way forward. It's easier to see the ray of light in darkness.
When the time is on you, start and the pressure is off.	If you don't know where to begin, just begin. When you have a deadline and feel the pressure of getting something done, the way to release the pressure is to simply begin. Just do it!
Understand through compassion or you will misunderstand the times.	We are all connected. Keep your heart open. Resist the need to go into the mind and the ego. Walk in another's shoes.
Vibrate the cosmos and the cosmos shall clear the path.	Repeat the words and thoughts that correspond to the things you consider "highest." Your self-conception automatically begins to change. Priorities evolve. Your path clears and your confidence to act manifests.

Tips for Stepping into Your Becoming:

1. Stop the chaos of the mind and tune to the divine.
2. Find your power in powerlessness.
3. Share your message before you depart.
4. See God in everything.

EXERCISE:

Practice any and all of this chapter. Describe and note your results here: ______________________________

PART 4

BEING

Perhaps you've heard the saying, "The only way out is through." Generally, as you awaken to your full beingness there are fewer words that will really describe the simplicity of being there. Form dissolves into formlessness and everything takes on a kind of circular nature. You have walked the path, stepped into your truth, found the essence of yourself, generally known the tools that work for you and those that don't, and have realized the wholeness to the whole.

"You've been walking in circles, searching.
Don't drink from the water's edge.
Throw yourself in.
Become the water.
Only then will your thirst end."

— *Jeanette Berson*

Once you open up to compassion and love in yourself, you begin to see it in others. Pretty soon judgments fall away, and no matter what the situation, you feel compassion for the experience or the experiencer. A kind of beingness takes over that is a balance between trust, faith, and knowing you are a part of a larger whole. The situations around you don't necessarily change, but your attitude about, or relationship with, them does. You become mindful in your life approach.

AWAKEN — TRANSFORM — REALIZE

Chapter 12

Living in the Now

"If you are depressed, you are living in the past.
If you are anxious, you are living in the future.
If you are at peace, you are living in the present."

— Lao Tzu

Mindful nonjudgmental awareness of the moment we are living in might be the best way to live in the now. Mindfulness is at the heart of Buddhism, Taoism, and many Native American traditions—not to mention yoga. It takes intentional practice to override life's distractions to awaken to the moment. To live in the moment, or now, means being conscious, aware, and in the present with all of your senses. It means not dwelling on the past, nor being anxious or worrying about the future.

"If you have one eye on yesterday,
and one eye on tomorrow,
you're going to be cockeyed today."

— Anonymous

Mindfulness means maintaining a moment-by-moment awareness of our thoughts, feelings, bodily sensations, and surrounding environment. When you are mindful, you are more likely to see yourself as a part of the whole of humanity or the universe. The Buddhist monks talk about "being one with everything." In fact, practicing that concept is how I got through my shamanic ayahuasca plant medicine ceremony a few years back without barfing! Everyone else was. But I saw that I was no different than the plant I was ingesting. I saw that we were one. I saw a kind of oneness with no separation or ego. And stepping outside of your ego and self-consciousness can help you avoid worrying, too. We can get trapped in the past or present and very easily miss the now. When we concentrate our attention on the present, we focus on the task at hand. We give our full attention to what we are doing, and we let go of outcomes. Mindfulness also involves a kind of acceptance, meaning you pay attention to your thoughts and feelings without judging them—without believing that there's a "right" or "wrong" way to think or feel in a given moment. Rather than rehashing the past or imagining the future, when we practice mindfulness, our thoughts tune into what we're sensing in the present moment.

This may sound crazy, but when I first moved to Maui, I thought about how much my ex-husband would like it here. I failed to see that I was with Patrick and my ex was many years in my past. I had forgotten I was supposed to be living in the present. In fact, when I travelled through Central and South America doing healing work, I thought about how much my ex would gain from such a trip. I imagined us working it out and him traveling with me on my next trip. But he was busy in his life with other lovers, never looking back in an effort to work things out with me. I was still wounded from the past. Only when I stopped thinking like that was I finally healed. It went on for so many years, but eventually, the beliefs and feelings faded. I couldn't be present in myself, or in my life, for me or anyone else, until I stopped living in the past or bringing the past into my present. Nothing but time seemed to heal me from thinking my ex was a part of my life.

Similarly, when Shiitake was sick, I used to catch myself thinking about how I would forever be wounded on Maui because, in my future, everywhere I went would remind me of her sickness. When I caught myself thinking this way, I was better able to stop the mind chatter and be fully present with her during our last days together; a few days we even went up country above the lavender farm and danced in the mist. Dancing will always make you fully present in the now. She didn't always feel well enough to dance with me, but she smiled so big. Every time I think of or see the magical Maui mist, I see her smile coming through it like that of the Cheshire cat in *Alice in Wonderland*. Her smile will always be in the mist.

Alice:
You've gone quite mangy, cat...
but your grin's a comfort.

Cheshire Cat:
And you've picked up a bit of an attitude,
still curious and willing to learn, I hope.

At the points in my life when I was the most depressed I spent most of my time worrying about events that never even happened. Worrying means you are thinking about the future and have forgotten God. Patrick and I had many challenges in the beginning stages of our relationship. I spent much of the first part of our time on Maui resenting that I had spent several thousand dollars to move across the country, and then more to move to Maui. And he didn't seem to care that I had given up everything to be with him. I don't know what I expected him to do or say, but I began to resent him. Each time we had a disagreement, I started to think about packing my things and moving home. But where was home? I worried about where I was going to live and how I was going to pay for it and where I was going to get a job. The more I worried, the more I resented Patrick. When he would travel for work, I was left alone in the place he wanted to live. None of my family or friends were around. I was very alone. It didn't matter that I was on Maui. I could have been on any tropical island and I still would have been caught up in my dramas and traumas. We seemed to grow distant, and I was beginning to create the reality I was dreaming up in my mind. We forgot to appreciate the moments of today, and subliminally, we couldn't find the right way to forgive our past hurts; instead, we saw reflections of our pasts in each other.

Eventually, we confronted these issues and found that wounds from our past relationships were still haunting us. I learned to be even more comfortable with myself too. I had to be mindful and consciously breathe, asking myself whether I was okay in the now. How about you? Are you okay right now? At this moment? It's not really as bad as our mind makes it out to be, is it? When is the last time you smiled? Danced in the rain or mist?

Living consciously and mindfully decreases ego. And breathing deeply and consciously allows you to connect to what is happening now. The breath is always there with you. You don't have to be an expert to breathe. You just have to stop the chaos of the mind and be present.

I learned to do so by dedicating more time to my yoga practice and practicing mindfulness of the now.

I learned that seizing each moment in life allows us to prolong its value and make it more meaningful. Rather than seeking a quantity of time, when we live in the moment, we enjoy and savor every minute. We stop looking for the next exciting moment, person, or event. We can still set goals, but as we go about achieving them, we should be fully present, not focused on the end. That way we won't sacrifice quality for quantity.

Every day, my dogs remind me to live in the now. They don't think about what happened or what is going to happen. They teach me to live in each moment and embrace it for what it is. The other day, I was lying in bed with my pups when, suddenly, I started crying. I realized the special moment. I realized that our time together is short, the universe is big, and there we were. They were cuddled in my arms, warm and snoring. I realized all the things I worried about in life were suddenly gone, and it would be *this* moment that would go into my cellular memory as a positive and memorable experience of this lifetime. I realized that no matter what form my soul or spirit took on, it was this moment that would be present in my soul's blueprint. No matter what happened in the past or would happen in the future, I was content and so were they. I took a moment to notice the smells, sights, and sounds in the room. I was fully engaged and fully present. I was completely lost in the moment. I become very thankful for the moment, and that's when the tears came. I saw how loved I was. Nothing or no one will take that moment from me.

"Today me will live in the moment,
unless its unpleasant,
in which case me will eat a cookie."

— Cookie Monster

A quote by an unknown author says: "If you worry about what might be, and wonder what might have been, you will ignore what is." Sometimes, life gets too painful to exist within the moment. During the drama of Bella's rescue, my mind got the best of me. My thoughts told me what a bad person I was for letting her go over the cliff. Then that night before she was rescued I let my mind convince me she had fallen off the side to her death. I even heard her yelp as I imagined her tumbling over. But I learned that I didn't want to manifest those thoughts. I needed to be very clearly in the now in order to call for help and not do anything too hasty to risk my own life. I learned that staying in the moment requires recognizing the difference between the "what-ifs" and the what *is*. Projecting into the future is great if you are using it to achieve goals, but taking that projection and moving all facets (emotions and senses) into the present can help it manifest in the present. During Bella's rescue, I started to imagine that I was going to take her to her scheduled vet appointment in a few days and that she would be just fine. Miraculously, once she was rescued, she didn't have a single wound and needed *no* veterinary care. Although she was a bit of a celebrity at the vet's office that day.

You can have your consciousness consumed in your mind with worry, thinking, and what ifs, but you must believe you can find stillness; then you can take over your mind. Being in the body is a powerful tool for accessing the now. Yoga, for instance, will break the blocks to your thinking and put you back into your body. That's why I love it. If your reality is based on past events, the body believes that those things in your mind are happening now. Energy doesn't flow freely. When we do yoga, we break up the blocks and challenge the mind and body in a kind of reprogramming or training.

Essential oils and peaceful music can also help bring you into an awareness of now. An exercise I often practice when there is a kind of drama in my life is that I ask myself: "Am I okay right now?" Then I assess the situation and realize I'm just caught in my ego. There is something I want or expect and it's not going as I expected it to. I stop and realize that God has a different plan and know that I might need to have patience for a resolution to occur. Where is your mind? Past? Present? Future? What techniques can you use to be here now? Can you be here now with reverence and patience, and let go of expectation?

Tips for Stepping Into Your Becoming:

1. Stop thinking only about yourself.
2. This moment right here, right now is your life—live it!
3. Savor the present moment.
4. Smile.
5. It doesn't matter what you used to be; it's who you've become that matters most.
6. Uncertainty is a part of life so learn to be comfortable from within.
7. Breathe/meditate/do yoga.
8. Eat slowly and savor your food.

9. Lose track of time.
10. Dream about the future but work hard today.
11. Forgive past hurts.
12. See today as a gift—tomorrows are not guaranteed.
13. Accept what is bothering you and make peace with it.
14. Forgive yourself for not knowing something.
15. Release the phrase, "But that's how we've always done it."
16. Do the Buddhist Loving-Kindness Meditation.
17. Stop worrying about the future or dwelling on the past.
18. Make the current moment so beautiful it will be worth remembering.
19. Remove possessions from your life that remind you of your past.

EXERCISE:

What is important about this moment right now? ________________

____

____

____

Before you go to bed think of one thing you are grateful for in each day. What were you grateful for today? ______________________

____

____

____

How does this quote by the Buddha make you feel about the right now? "Since everything is a reflection of our minds, everything can be changed by our minds." ______________________________

____

____

____

____

Ask yourself, "What have I done with what God has given me?" How does this question make you feel about your right now? What can you do to change any negative thinking of the past and channel it into positive actions today? ______________________________

____

____

____

____

____

Have you let your ego get in your way today? Did you blame someone for something and not take responsibility for it yourself? Take a moment and think about the needs and challenges of another person you may have had a disagreement with, how your expectations got in the way, and how you could apologize or not overreact the next time. Were you projecting into the future? What about that present moment caused you to react? Where is your wound? ____________

____

____

____

____

____

____

AWAKEN — TRANSFORM — REALIZE

Chapter 13

Patience

"Have patience,
God isn't finished yet."

— Philippians 1:6

We live in a time of instant gratification, but not all things in life happen at record speed. Many people tend to lose faith or force solutions when things don't happen quickly enough. One thing I was taught early on in my shamanic training was that I must "trust the process." Apparently the process can take some time. In fact, I was told by my teachers to pull a card from my favorite oracle deck each day for patience. I'm so happy they told me that and even happier that I did it for several years. Of course, ironically, I couldn't get to the cards fast enough!

A divine order exists that organizes, plans, and knows when to bring something into fruition in your life. It's like the mustard seed. Before it can turn into something, it must be planted, watered, bud, and mature. Before we came into this life, we worked to co-create an intelligence with the divine called the higher self. Our higher self knows when to deliver what we are awaiting. When we are silent in ourselves, we can self-source the when and how to some degree. We came into this physical experience with blinders on—we forced ourselves to forget what we had planned so that life would be full of surprises that would allow us to establish faith in a presence that is coordinating on our behalf. Part of the journey is resting in our faith. And without patience, you can never fully understand the meaning of divine timing.

We've talked about being visionary and dreaming your world into being; you may see in your mind that which you wish to accomplish. This is what becomes your intention. There is, however, the question of when. Divine timing is not something that can be pushed to be made faster. What manifests and when is based on what is best for the highest good of all involved. The ego wants it to happen now. Forcing will cause certain portions of the whole to feel off. In divine right timing and divine will, all pieces will be like a miracle and feel effortless. Everything must be turned over to divine masters and guides to come to fruition.

For ten years, I wanted to write my first book, but it was not meant to be until recently. And for just about that same time span I have seen a home I was told I would live in. I was told that once I wrote the book, I would live there, but now I have written the book and I still don't live there. In fact, we are awaiting financing on a different house at present. I'm writing this second book now and I still don't live there. So perhaps there is another book? Perhaps it's not the book that needs to be written to live in the home, but at some point thereafter, I will live in it. I know that I can't currently afford this beautiful, large, ocean cliff-side home, but maybe God has another plan? I don't live each day thinking that something I will do will manifest it today, or even at all, but I do often wonder whether it is a dream or a reality. Still, I know that if it is meant to be, I will live there. I know I will always receive that which aligns with my highest good.

I know that God will give me my daily bread…
When I run after what I think I want,
My days are a furnace of distress and anxiety;
If I sit in my own place of patience,
What I need flows to me,
And without any pain.
From this I understand that
What I want also wants me,
Is looking for me
And attracting me;
When it cannot attract me
Any more to go to it,
It has to come to me.
There is a great secret
In this for anyone
Who can grasp it.

— Rumi

Our patience often reveals the degree of trust we have in God's timing. We can get caught up in our stories and forget to surrender to a larger vision. Each time we take the right actions, we are actually taking a step toward greater awareness.

"Whatever comes of itself, let it come."

— Paramhansa Yogananda

Yogananda used this phrase to describe the right attitude for dealing with what life brings you—failure or success, poverty or wealth, sickness or health—just let it come, but do not let what comes define you or determine your happiness. If you live centered within your Self, then whatever does come cannot change your inner happiness. Life will bring you many ups and downs. According to the Bible, patience is a spiritual fruit, and according to scripture, God is pleased with us when we display this virtue. Many verses state this truth:

"Be still before the LORD and wait patiently for Him."

— Psalm 37:7

"God is good to those who wait for Him."

— Lamentations 3:25

"God often uses trials to strengthen our patience, allowing our Christian faith to mature and become complete."

— James 1:3-4

"And we know that all things—including these difficult trials—work out for the good of those who love God."

— Romans 8:28

"God does indeed hear the cries of His children and will answer those cries according to His perfect will and timing. A righteous man may have many troubles; the LORD delivers him from them all."

— Psalm 34:18-19

"The plans God has for His children are good plans— to help us, not hurt us."

— Jeremiah 29:11

Buddhist Approach

Buddhist teacher Pema Chodron counsels on patience. She teaches that patience means waiting to act or speak until you can do so without causing harm. "Patience has a quality of enormous honesty in it," she said. The Zen monks are taught to be patient and to endure. They are also taught that patience requires positive emotion and that patience is needed to further our own spiritual growth and to help others grow. This means great patient effort, enduring effort, persistent and consistent effort is greater and more noble than the violent effort of frustration and anger—and it is also more successful. This sort of effort persists day after day, during good times and bad times, understands and uses the Law of Karma (where actions have consequences). This enduring effort in skillfulness of body, speech, mind, persistent effort in ethics, meditation, and study is said to bring about spiritual progress.

In the Buddhist practices, patience is necessary if we are to progress spiritually. Patience toward the natural world, toward ourselves, and, of course, toward others lessens suffering. It is believed that the more we seek comfort in our lives and preciously treat ourselves, the less we are able to endure any discomfort or hardship, and, therefore, we create more potentiality for suffering and distress. The spiritual life is not easy. It requires discipline and an ability to endure suffering and distress. Change produces discomfort, and if we shy away from discomfort, we will shy away from change.

We need to be patient with ourselves. This means being patient with our bodies—and with our spiritual progress. To live a spiritual life and make spiritual progress, there are a few points we should bear in mind:

1. Develop positive routines or habits and be disciplined. Be regular and consistent in your practice.
2. Expect difficulties and become aware of resistance to spiritual growth and spiritual practice.
3. Don't project your internal conflict onto others.
4. Don't get frustrated when you have a measure for success and you are not achieving milestones. You have just become more conscious.
5. Learn to live happily with impermanence and change. To change is to move beyond current attachments.
6. Don't look for powerful experiences. This is a wrong way of thinking about the spiritual life. As you progress on your spiritual path, there will be less discrepancy between you and a "powerful spiritual experience." You may have strong experiences in meditation

from time to time, and they may give you faith that there are states of consciousness beyond what you usually experience, but don't get distracted by these experiences or start to chase after them. Strong or powerful experiences in meditation are an occasional byproduct of the spiritual life for some, but they are not what the spiritual life is about. What is important is what sort of person you are becoming and how you behave or behave toward other people.

7. Develop and maintain an attitude of goodwill toward yourself. Be patient with yourself. Fundamentally, you are all right. Just keep making an effort. Self-love is the grounding we need for all obstacles.
8. Exercise patience with others—particularly be patient with their faults and failings. Be patient with difference. Sometimes others are just different from us and we interpret that as a failing on their part. We get annoyed with them.

There were moments on my spiritual path where I'd ask things like "What's the point?" and "Why am I doing all this self-improvement?" and after all the aha moments with big awakenings happening, I was left wondering, "What's next?" I was impatient for the next aha and big transformative experience. But then I realized that as I was growing more connected—not so much increasing my vibration, but shaking out all my non-serving beliefs—I reacted less and felt that things seemed to be less dramatic all around. I became aware that through awareness and a shifting of consciousness, this situation was as it should be. There should be less that shocked me because in the new awareness, all things were becoming part of the same God, the same divine. I didn't need to be impatient for more measures of success to be proven to me in my expanded state.

Be very aware when people tell you they had, or will have, a huge transformation, or powerful initiation because it is a sign of their disconnectedness from the whole or they are just very new on the path of spiritual transformation and awakening. It's not a bad thing, but those on a self-serving path to awakening are likely just in the early stages of awakening. I have spent much time there myself.

Much of our lives, we experience ourselves as the center of the universe, and from this standpoint, we can get hurt, upset, and angry when others don't seem to be going along with our ideals. In order to develop patience toward others, we need to get beyond selfishness and begin to see that real self-interest includes the interests of others. Having or developing practices of patience can be a challenging act in understanding, compassion, love, and kindness.

"To understand all is to forgive all."

— French proverb

AWAKEN — TRANSFORM — REALIZE

Chapter 14

Leadership

"A leader is best when people barely know he exists,
when his work is done, his aim fulfilled,
they will say: we did it ourselves."

— Lao Tsu

Many times in my life I have wished for a mentor to appear. When I was younger, and starting my corporate career, I sought out a business mentor to take me under her wing and show me how to be the best person I could be. I never had any luck, and I began to doubt the existence of such a person. I read all the self-help business books and practiced their teachings when I could. I was ready to change the world, but all those who had already put in their time were not in support of my young, naive, optimistic, and enthusiastic ways. I knew there was an art to the application, and I figured eventually I'd learn what that was. I became a student without a teacher.

As I went on my spiritual journey, which really began for me in 2006,

I sought out a group, a method, a formula, and a technique that could show me the way. As I stepped into yoga and into Shamanism, I found that "system or method" to some extent, but I took every class I could and when I reached the end of each one, I still wanted more. I wanted to go right to the source, so I jumped on a plane to Peru to work directly with the shaman. But after a few trips, I grew disappointed that they kept teaching and healing in the same ways when I thought the practices were broader. I knew there was more, so I began to contemplate the concept of self-sourcing. If I wanted to know more, I had to go to the source of that source.

I found very few people on my path who could play the role of mentor for me. I watched teachers teach with physical and emotional pains (showing their human flaws), and others with huge egos who were seeking out some kind of self-promoting fiefdom. As my awareness and consciousness expanded, I began to keep an eye open for a guru of sorts. I found I was intrigued with the shaman, and one or two advanced yogis and swamis, but honestly, I found no one whose power was greater than my own. I wasn't being big-headed about it. It was just an observation. I then noted that we came from the same source, and whatever these others were accessing was the same source I could access. I just needed to learn how.

When I exhausted all the classroom time, I had no choice but to become self-sourcing, and I realized that was God's plan for me, for all of us. I also realized that to teach something meant that I had to keep myself abreast of the teachings. When no one else taught me, I learned to seek and find answers on my own. I even forced myself to teach in hopes of learning more. But I wasn't doing it entirely for the joy of teaching. I grew frustrated about this in my past, but I am thankful for it today—very thankful! I will admit, though, that I felt I might have gotten caught up in my ego at a few points on my seeker's journey since I'm only human. It was the competitive nature in me. I thought maybe I was just convincing myself I didn't need a teacher, but I was also aware of the mirror. I was aware that if I needed a teacher, I would have more need to have one. I was aware that if I truly believed I didn't need one, then I would not have one. But I eventually realized that taking the classes was really just the start of my training. But I was also intrigued with the idea of having my own guru. I prayed for many years on my spiritual path that a mentor would show up, and a few came and went. They taught me their lessons, and they told me I would be a great shaman as a result of my life experiences. Or they would tell me I was balanced and would find my way.

I was beginning to see a kind of parallel with becoming the teachings and stepping up to tell others about what I was learning in a kind of leadership role. I saw that many leaders didn't have spiritual backgrounds, and they were leading unethically, without principles and morals. I was led to know more about spiritual leadership in other regions of the world because, to me, leadership is not some mean bossy dude in a boardroom or someone screaming on the other end of the phone telling me what to do. A leader is someone who takes ownership of self.

I tend to find the most intriguing people are those who seem to have a certain worldliness about them, a kind of deep knowledge. Such people can lead with strength and conviction because they have energetically, empathically, and emotionally connected to a need or desire and want to assist in fulfilling that with divine assistance or the voice of God on their shoulders. I began to think that leadership without a spiritual connection is that bossy dude running his mouth and thinking out loud, but being led and listening to the divine in business or life, having compassion for all living beings in a united purpose could change everything. So I began to take a deeper dive into spiritual concepts on leadership.

If you were to become a leader with a spiritual background, you might be called a spiritual leader or a guru. You might even simply be called a coach. Either way, being a spiritual person in life, business, your church, or discipline inherently makes you someone who can guide others through life's trials. The Bible says a spiritual leader possesses the "spiritual gift of leadership" and has the ability to lead others as a direct result of the gifts received from, and performed by, the power of the Holy Spirit. But all leaders lead by example, and the good ones serve others before serving themselves.

Leadership is not about having followers! A leader is concerned with the souls around him. To be a guru of something means to be a teacher of that thing. It basically means taking what is dark (ignorance) and turning it to the light (the divine). It means being the importer of knowledge, to raise or lift up. Yogi Bhajan talked about this, suggesting that to master something was to teach it. It's easy to be a student of life. However, it takes guts to get up in front of others and admit you don't know everything, but you are willing to teach what you do know. This is how the ego serves us. We don't want to look like we don't know something, so we learn everything we can in order to teach others. We must also gain practical hands-on experience, and with dedication and time, we can become masters…or is that master teachers? But if we take that a step farther, we can channel into the divine and guide from a pure place that goes beyond our current world experiences and become a leader with compassion and a channeled pipeline into the divine. And what if we created more teachers and less followers? What if we made smarter students than teachers?

Religion and spirituality are difficult to define in definite terms. Spirituality and religion go hand-in-hand—the only difference is that while religion is an organized system that pays homage to a god, spirituality does not always need a deity to define the parameters of the person's spiritual conduct. Patrick and I have had this discussion, and because he is a Christian, I think it's a bit hard for him to understand that I believe in Jesus and know that he is the Son of God, but I also believe all of us are the sons and daughters of God and that there are many other avatars such as Jesus who have been a part of many other cultures and backgrounds. After all, Jesus wasn't a Christian. It's also my belief that if we all opted for a more "spiritual approach," we might just all get along better.

Over the years, I have noticed that many who walk the path into enlightenment find their way and want to spread their message, but in the sharing is a kind of territorial—for lack of better words—pissing match that happens when someone doesn't become fully enlightened. We are sort of caught in this place right now where people are moving from the Picean Age into the Aquarian Age but are still exhibiting many Picean Age attributes. I came across a woman the other day on Facebook who was complaining that she, as a lightworker, was upset that her new friend was copying and pasting her words on her page and claiming them as her own. The way I figure any truly enlightened "lightworker" to share her message would be to do so wholeheartedly, meaning what it said, regardless of who claimed ownership over it. When we are yet to go through the process fully of awakening, we get bits and pieces of divine messages that come in, and they are so good that we want to own them as our own. The reality is that all of the concepts, tools, humanity—they've all been around for eons. There really isn't much new except for the way we look at things or the amount of enlightenment we let in or choose to own or share. I think this is where the good leaders emerge. Whether someone claims to be a messenger of the divine or not, a few beings have gotten out of their own ways and stepped into the spotlight to take leadership roles. It's almost as if they would have exploded or internally combusted if they hadn't. Incredible messages spew from their being, and many want to know why or how. Some create followers, but the good ones create leaders and teachers. By the example they set, we are moved to make change happen where it is needed and to create peace where there is war.

Throughout history, many have played the roles of both spiritual and religious leaders. Some did exemplary work with such dedication that their work, and they themselves, were recognized the world over for their steadfast dedication and wisdom. Let's take a look at these gurus as a concept, overall keeping in mind how a better leadership role could be played by each of us.

Guru Leadership

"When the student is ready the teacher will appear."

— Buddhist proverb

Our planet has been visited by rare individuals whose sole purpose is the spiritual uplifting of humanity. And by spiritual, I mean a kind of meaningful or blissful experience, joined in spirit and closely akin in interests, attitude, and outlook to sacred matters. These Spiritual Masters have been called by different names, at different times, in different countries. They have been referred to as: Living Master, Avatar, Enlightened One, Savior, Messiah, Divine Mother, Messenger, Guru, Living Saint, and the like. They came to offer us what has been called: Enlightenment, Awakening, Realization, Liberation, or Salvation. The words used may be different, but in essence, these masters all came to do the same thing—awaken dormant spiritual knowledge within their pupils. This is the kind of leader I want to be, to look up to, or be guided by. How about you? Let's take a look at a few traditions. Some get a bit deep, so bear with me.

Hindu Traditions

In Hinduism, a great importance is placed on finding a guru who can share transcendental knowledge and enlighten the mind of her students. A satguru is a true teacher. In the presence of the satguru, knowledge flourishes (Gyana raksha), sorrow diminishes (Dukha kshaya), joy wells up without any reason (Sukha aavirbhava), abundance dawns (Samriddhi), and all talents manifest (Sarva samvardhan). Pretty cool, huh? But, any way you put it, the guru is basically a teacher who imparts wisdom. It's been said that Jesus Christ fits the Hindu definition and characteristics of a guru.

Paramahansa Yogananda was an Indian yogi and guru who introduced millions of Westerners to the teachings of meditation and Kriya Yoga through his book *Autobiography of a Yogi.* In his youth, he sought out many of India's Hindu sages and saints, hoping to find an illuminated teacher to guide him in his spiritual quest. The following is what he shared on the role of a guru in one's spiritual search. I find these words relevant as we begin this discussion because sometimes we call out for help when something is not working. What if someone heard your request and came to help?

> *Within your heart cry constantly for God. When you have convinced the Lord of your desire for Him, He will send someone—your guru—to teach you how to know Him. Only he who knows God can show others how to know Him. When I found such a one, my guru Swami Sri Yukteswarji, I realized that God doesn't teach through mystery, but through illumined souls. God is invisible, but He becomes visible through the intelligence and spiritual perception of one who is in constant communion with Him. There may be many teachers in one's life, but there is only one guru. In the guru-disciple relationship a divine law is fulfilled, as demonstrated even in the life of Jesus, when he acknowledged John the Baptist as his guru.*

*

> *He alone who is God-realized, and who has been commanded by God to redeem souls, is a guru. One cannot be a guru merely by thinking he is. Jesus showed that the true guru acts solely at God's behest, when he said: "No man can come to me, except the Father which hath sent me draw him." He gave all credit to the power of God. If a teacher is without egotism, you may know that God alone resides in his body temple; and when you tune in with him you are in tune with God. Jesus reminded his disciples: "Whosoever shall receive me, receiveth not me, but Him that sent me.*

The true guru has no desire to place himself in the hearts of others, but rather to awaken in their consciousness, the consciousness of God."

*

Such a guru, ordained by God to help individuals in response to their deep prayers, is not an ordinary teacher; but is a human vehicle whose body, speech, mind, and spirituality God uses as a channel to attract and guide lost souls back to His home of immortality. We meet various teachers in the beginning, through our vague desire to know truth. But a guru is a living embodiment of scriptural truth and an agent of salvation appointed by God in response to a devotee's incessant petitions for release from the bondage of matter.

The Guru Gita (verse 17) describes the guru as "dispeller of darkness" (from gu, "darkness," and ru, "that which dispels"). It also says a true, God-illumined guru is one who, in his attainment of self-mastery, has realized his identity with the omnipresent Spirit. Such an individual is uniquely qualified to lead the seeker on his or her inward journey toward perfection.

"Only a master, one who knows God,
may rightly teach others about Him.
To regain one's divinity one must have such a master or guru.
He who faithfully follows a true guru becomes like him, for the guru helps to elevate the disciple to his own level of realization."

— The Guru Gita (verse 17)

A true guru's goal, ordained by God, who has been commanded by God to redeem souls, to serve as a channel, is to help people. Yogananda felt that the guru-disciple relationship is the highest expression of friendship, and it is based on unconditional divine love and wisdom and is among the most sacred of all relationships. He believed that those who partake of this relationship are on the way to wisdom and freedom.

"Acquire the transcendental knowledge from a Self-realized master
by humble reverence, by sincere inquiry, and by service.
The wise ones who have realized the
Truth will impart the Knowledge to you.

— Bhagavad Gita

Hindu and Buddhist Traditions

The Hindu and Buddhist traditions honor their teachers through the Indian festival of Guru Purnima. This celebration is dedicated to thanking spiritual and academic teachers because these traditions believe gurus to be the most necessary part of life. Puja (worship) is offered on this day to pay respect to a guru or spiritual guide. On this day, Shiva became the first guru (Adi Guru) in the Indian traditions, and yoga began with the birth of this first spiritual master.

> *The story goes that over 15,000 years ago, a yogi appeared in the upper regions of the Himalayas. Nobody knew what his origins were. But his presence was extraordinary, and people gathered. However, he exhibited no signs of life, but for the occasional tears of ecstasy that rolled down his face. People be-*

> *gan to drift away, but seven men stayed on. When he opened his eyes, they pleaded with him, wanting to experience whatever was happening to him. He dismissed them, but they persevered. Finally, he gave them a simple preparatory step and closed his eyes again. The seven men began to prepare. Days rolled into weeks, weeks into months, months into years, but the yogi's attention did not fall upon them again.*
>
> *After eighty-four years of sadhana (ritual or discipline toward a spiritual goal), on the summer solstice that marks the advent of Dakshinayana, the earth's southern run (the six-month period between the summer and winter solstice), the yogi looked at them again. They had become shining receptacles, wonderfully receptive. He could not ignore them anymore. On the very next full moon day, the yogi turned south and sat as a guru to these seven men. The Adiyogi (the first yogi) thus became the Adi Guru. Adiyogi expounded these mechanics of life for many years. The seven disciples became celebrated as the Saptarishis and took this knowledge across the world.*
>
> *Guru Purnima is held sacred in the yogic tradition because the Adiyogi opened up the possibility for a human being to evolve consciously. The seven different aspects of yoga that were put in these seven individuals became the foundation for the seven basic forms of yoga, something that has still endured.*[1]

Volumes have been written on the rituals to worship the guru. It is believed many gurus are responsible for assisting in the soul's liberation.

---

1 Source: http://en.wikipedia.org/wiki/Guru_Purnima

If your soul were liberated, wouldn't you think you'd be a better student, teacher, or leader? Some traditions believe that Guru, God, and Self (the soul) are the same. In Theravada Buddhism, the teacher is not generally considered to be a guru, but rather (and as Yogananda said) a spiritual friend. In Tibetan Buddhism, the guru is seen as the Bodhisattva (someone with great knowledge and awareness), and it is believed that without a teacher, there can be no experience of insight.

"Rely on the teachings to evaluate a guru:
Do not have blind faith, but also no blind criticism."

— Dalai Lama

The role of a spiritual teacher or guru is often misunderstood in the West. We have lost the ancient system of studying under one teacher for many years to learn a craft, and we are not used to this system anymore. We are in a hurry to get ahead, to be the boss, and to make the big paycheck. There is a lot of confusion about spiritual teachers. In Buddhism, the teacher is said to lead you to your own inner wisdom—your own 'inner guru,' so you can develop your own wisdom and insight to become a teacher or leader.

"To find a Buddha, all you have to do is see your nature. Your nature is the Buddha. And the Buddha is the person who's free: free of plans, free of cares. If you don't see your nature and run around all day looking somewhere else, you'll never find a Buddha. The truth is, there's nothing to find. But to reach such an understanding, you need a teacher, and you need to struggle to make yourself understand."

— Bodidharma (fifth century Chinese monk)

The reasons to follow a guru are many, but generally, one follows a guru on the spiritual path to have someone guide him or her on finding the right way. And the best person to guide is someone who has already successfully travelled the path. Sounds like a great leader, right? There are four kinds of lama (teachers) in Tibetan Buddhism. The individual teacher who is the holder of the lineage, the teacher who is the word of the Buddhas, the symbolic teacher of all appearances, and the absolute teacher; the true nature of mind. So perhaps we need to understand this concept in terms of the multitude of leaders we must have as well—each with unique and various disciplines. There is generally a list of qualifications for finding a teacher, or guru, of the basic philosophies and, from there, there is a bit of an expectation that you will no longer need a teacher but will become your own teacher or even become your own Buddha. Imagine if leadership in all aspects worked like this. Imagine if business schools across the nation taught any of these philosophies or practices to create great future leaders in our society. Imagine if the qualifications for teachers looked something like this:

- must have proper ethical behavior and not harm others but try to help
- have single-pointed concentration
- have no self-grasping or egoistic thoughts
- love and compassion are main motivations to teach
- have a proper intellectual understanding of realized emptiness
- have a perseverance in teaching
- hold a wealth of scriptural knowledge

- be more learned and realized than their students
- be a skilled speaker
- have no disappointment in the performance of your students

Just imagine an education system with those kinds of values—and then a business world composed of professionals who were taught in such a system. It would be Utopia!

Sikh Traditions

In Sikhism, the guru is the source of all knowledge. Kundalini yoga often parallels the Sikh traditions. In my personal practice, I have found the true essence of Kundalini yoga is that it breaks down blocks or barriers that keep you from full on self-discovery and self-mastery. It's not called the "yoga of awareness" for nothing! A Sikh (Punjabi) is a follower of Sikhism, a monotheistic religion that originated during the fifteenth century in the Punjab region of South Asia. The term "Sikh" has its origin in the Sanskrit word meaning "disciple" or "student" or "instruction." The religion is all about the relationship between the teacher and the student. The core belief is in One God and the lessons of ten eternal living gurus (teachers/leaders) who lived from 1469 until 1708.

The shabads or hymns of the *Guru Granth Sahib* are known as Gurbani (the guru's word), and are written in the Gurmukhi script and composed in raag, a musical score. The main focus of any Sikh worship service is kirtan, or singing the sacred shabads of Gurbani. Shabads may be sung by kirtanis (individual singers) or ragis (professional singers versed in Gurbani) accompanied by sangat (members of the Sikh congregation). Sometimes in the yoga community, you will hear people talking of the sangat as a way of honoring the group as a whole—teachers and students. You might here this term used in a yoga community.

Sikhs must believe in the following values: equality, personal right to life with certain duties, doing good deeds, remembering God, living a family life, sharing 10 percent of net earnings with charity, accepting God's will, accepting the four truths of life: truth, contentment, contemplation, and naam (in the name of God). Sikhs also live with The Three Pillars of Sikh belief: 1) Naam Japo: meditation, singing of hymns from the *Guru Granth Sahib* or of the various names of God, especially the chanting of the word "waheguru" (basically meaning "Wow! God is amazing!"); 2) Kirat Karo is to earn an honest, pure, and dedicated living by exercising one's God-given skills, abilities, talents, and hard labor for the benefit and improvement of the individual, one's family, and society at large. 3) And, finally, Vand Chhako is to share what you have and to consume it together as a community, whether it is wealth, food, etc. The term is also used to mean to share one's wealth with others in the community, to give to charity, to distribute langar (a community meal), and in general, to help others.

I felt it was important to share the Sikh traditions here because I believe they are so misunderstood, and as a practitioner of Kundalini yoga, I am very proud to be a part of such a great community. If any aspect of this or any of the above traditions were brought into our Western ways, I believe we'd live happier and holier lives with more value and compassion placed on others and less on our materialistic American ways.

"Some of you who are sitting here will become great Teachers of the Age of Aquarius. You must understand that you have to build your character first. Care for yourself, be kind to yourself, be compassionate to yourself. That is what you have to do."

— Yogi Bhajan

Yogi Bhajan often said he came to create teachers, not to gather students. He saw every student as a potential teacher. He developed a worldwide network of teachers who heal others with their kindness, compassion, and a lot of Kundalini yoga and meditation. He felt everyone is a student, and everyone is a teacher, and if you are striving to live a healthy, happy, and holy life, you can do that and become an example and guide to others. He felt an Aquarian age teacher could be a kind of forklift for the soul, a lighthouse of hope, an institution of integrity, trust, and humility.

"People are in pain, and they need the pain alleviated.
They need to know that you can see that pain.
If a person is hungry, first feed him.
To a starving person, food is God.
Once he is satisfied and a little secure,
he can consider the possibility that God is food.
The ability to apply consciousness will make you a good teacher."

— Yogi Bhajan

In the Western World

In the U.S., we have a very different view of leadership, and it tends to be more about making money and taking from others, versus serving or giving back. Of course, that's a bit of a generalization, but our leaders generally have no qualifications other than a college education likely being preferred. Mindfulness with roots in any kind of spiritual study is so important for great leaders. Our materialistic American society is beginning to fail in many ways. Leaders need to be well-rounded in many disciplines, and since we all come from the same source, it would seem most natural to connect to that source to guide others.

We need to change our understanding and attitude about leadership. We need to have a depth of experience to be something we claim to be. What you claim to be should be natural, a living experience. Self-awareness of one's presence must be understood to lead others. You must learn to listen and decide when something in your consciousness is right…or wrong. Don't play games. As a society, we need to take responsibility for self. We have to understand, love, and trust each other as one, rather than being in competition. We must practice being in a neutral mind and leading from a place of united oneness.

"The sun shines on everyone.
It doesn't make choices.
When it rain it rains on everyone
It doesn't make choices.
The one spirit lives in everyone.
It doesn't make choices.
We pray, we pray for everyone.
We don't make choices."

— *Snatam Kaur*

Oneness

A true leader understands the full concept of oneness and leads from the heart. Quantum physics experts are now starting to prove what many energy workers and intuitives have known for a long time—all things are connected to the same stuff! When all things are broken down to their most basic form, they are shown to consist of the same stuff—energy, one energy! In other words, we all exist in an infinite kind of soup. No matter what the matter is—it's all a bunch of the same sameness. So if everything is energy, then it is merely a vibrating mass that joins together with other harmonious frequencies to form what we perceive as reality, what we experience in the physical world. So if all this energy is the same, and it makes you and me a reality, then it means we are much more alike than we are different.

So here is where quantum physics starts to get pretty cool...everyone and everything before or after us is also the same. It means that the past, present, and future all exist in that same soup. It means that all knowledge is also a part of the same sameness. Therefore, all enlightened masters and teachers also exist there and so does their knowledge. We really are not just all one, but we have access to everything! So perhaps now is a great time to revisit self-sourcing?

We all have a kind of sixth sense. And we all have an ability to access this information all the time. Now imagine combining the concept of the mirror with the concept of oneness...Are we really a mirror of oneness? Of God? Are we truly the light of God? Are we God? So the idea that we can create our world as we want it doesn't sound so far-fetched after all, does it?

"Science without religion is lame,
religion without science is blind."

— Albert Einstein

Tips for Stepping Into Your Becoming:

1. Don't lose faith. God has a plan.
2. Patience reveals the degree of trust we have in God's timing.
3. Live centered within Self.
4. Be a Guru before being a leader.
5. A teacher is a leader.
6. Be a teacher with divine principles.
7. Lead from a place of oneness.
8. Become a mirror of God.

EXERCISE:

I have a passion to learn, and when I do learn, I love to share what I know as honestly as I can. How about you? Are you afraid to share what you know? What would be the worst thing that could happen to you if you did share what you know? What do you know that you could teach? Do you have a passion for mastering any subject? If so, what would you like to master? To teach? ____________________

____

____

____

____

EXERCISE: Meditation for the Neutral Mind

It is easy to hear a truth, but difficult to live it—to embed it deeply into your heart and mind. The Neutral Mind opens the gate to that deep remembrance of the self and soul. The Neutral Mind lives for the touch of vastness. It lets all other thoughts be without disturbance to your constant inner light.

Posture:

Sit in an easy pose (legs crossed) with your spine straight. Put both hands in your lap with your palms facing up. Rest your right hand in your left. The thumb tips may touch or not.

Eyes and Mental Focus:

Remove all tension from every part of your body. Sit straight by achieving a balance. Close your eyes. Imagine seeing yourself sitting peacefully and full of radiance. Then gradually let your energy collect like a flow at the brow point (at the base of the nose where the eyes meet).

Breath:

Let your breath regulate itself into a meditative, slow, almost suspended, manner.

Mantra:

Concentrate without effort at brow point and mentally vibrate in a simple monotone, as if chopping the sound, projecting each syllable distinctly:

Wha-hay gu-roo (Infinity identity from darkness to light)

Call on the Higher Self and keep going steadily through all barriers. Let go and let God.

Time:

Practice this meditation for three to thirty-one minutes at a session.

Note: It might seem odd, but the timing works on different aspects of the mind and body. The time varies with the technique. Various times affect the effects! Here is what they mean: (You can look up more about them, and find a few exercises, at http://www.3ho.org.)

- In 3 minutes, you affect your circulation and blood chemistry.
- In 11 minutes the pituitary gland and the nerves start to learn and change.
- In 22 minutes your three minds (negative, positive, and neutral) start to work together so your mental integration changes.
- 31 minutes affects your whole mind and your aura, and the 31 tattwas are balanced.
- 37½ minutes reflects from the whole aura to Infinity and back, stimulating the perception of Naad—the inner sound.
- In 62 minutes your "shadow mind" and your positive projection are integrated.
- 2½ hours completes the cycle of prana and apana so what you gain will hold through the cycle of the day. It holds change in the subconscious.

AWAKEN — TRANSFORM — REALIZE

Chapter 15

The Business of Healing

"Healing is a matter of time,
but it is sometimes also a matter of opportunity."

— Hippocrates

Knowing that we all exist in oneness is rather interesting in the space of healing. If we are all one, then isn't the need for healing the self greater? If we are all a bunch of the same sameness, then are we all really a big mess as a whole? We can all likely agree that we have a combined bunch of problems for which we need a solution.

We collaborate on the makeup of our world. In that collaboration, we have so many wounds, and either we are afraid to, don't know how to, or don't know we have the option to dream an amazing beautiful world into being. We have famine, sickness, heartbreak, financial struggles, and a general lack of connection with self, let alone with others. We have so much need for healing so we can collaboratively create a more conscious and beautiful world. But in the business of healing, just like in any business, the healer needs to make money to survive. Is it right that when someone cannot afford to be healed, our world struggles? How do we change this? I've always believed that rather than just doing a healing for someone, we need to strengthen our world by teaching how the healing works, so it's available to everyone; then we can offer more healing without the expectation of receiving anything in return… for the sake of our planet. But I also believe in an energy exchange for the service of healing. In fact, so did Yogi Bhajan. He used to sprinkle money outside the places he was teaching and charge an admission. Some took the money and came in, others just took the money. What would you do?

If our schools taught forms of healing or spirituality rather than so many other ridiculous things, we would grow up knowing we had the power to change our world, but instead, kids leave school with minimal direction and so much pressure to compete against each other when they could have learned to hold hands and collaboratively change the world. If yoga, or something like it, were taught in schools, it would help change the minds of our youth. Doesn't it make you wonder if we are intentionally being kept from such knowledge?

When the mind dwells in fear, sadness, embarrassment, anger, guilt, disgust, and other defensive and negative emotions, our stress increases and our ability to recover from stress or illness is also impaired. We learn to choose coping mechanisms, and our emotional habits begin to determine our experiences and create our personal world and the world around us. Yoga, for example, helps change the mind so it will create more neutral and positive emotions. Positive emotions change thought-patterns and allow for new responses that help us better cope under stress. And when we live stress-free, we are more clear about our destinies and gain internal confidence, contentment, and control through effortless effort. As Yogi Bhajan said, we should not necessarily focus on the promises of an afterlife, because we need to be the promise of life now.

Instead of experiencing unlimited consciousness, we reduce ourselves to self-imposed limitations and boundaries, and we fail to sync with the infinite. We lose self and forget that we incarnated to experience happiness. We forget that we are able to be happy because we get caught in our ego and our perceived wounds. We get so caught up in the story of our wounds that we forget to have gratitude for life and trust in the infinite and the creator. We think other people have to help us heal because they somehow possess a skill we do not. We all have the power to heal ourselves, even though we may not realize it. The true business of a healer is to show others how to heal self. If healers simply heal, then others become dependent upon them to heal when the next issue arrives. The goal for all should be learning how to heal self. Where are *you* going to start?

Sure, you may have lost your path, so healers, spiritual guides, and coaches can be used to help you find it, but so many of these helpers have yet to step outside of their egos to see clearly enough to provide the direction needed. It is when we step out of our egos that the circle of healing starts….

The Circle of Healing

Either we think something is wrong and we seek healing, or we think nothing is wrong with us until something happens that changes us and we seek answers. Either way, we go on the seeker's path to find purpose and meaning. We find glimpses of Self, and we begin to peel the layers down deeper until we reach some kind of plateau we are satisfied with; then another issue arises and we seek again, peeling yet deeper. We go through a cycle until we've repeated patterns of living and healing enough times to start taking notice, seek out solutions to our own problems, and eventually, heal ourselves by simply stepping into our own innate power. Then we reach another plateau where we think we are wise and have learned a lot. We step outside of our social circles of the wounded self and become more internal. Reaching a place of awareness, we begin to see that countless people are still spinning and spinning with new healing modalities or other tools to find self with the guidance of another who has yet to find an egoless self or true connection to the divine. (If we are truly lucky, we find a real, honest to goodness guru or ourself.)

The circle spins and spins until at some point a place is reached where all illusion falls away and we become self-sourcing and non-judgmental of each seeker's path (including our own) and we honor the process. All teachings fall away and a sense of being-ness unfolds. Before the being-ness takes full effect, it appears as if all the countless paths and tools to reach enlightenment are almost silly since no matter what path you choose, you are always on the correct path anyway. *You are always connected to the power that created you. The idea of wrong becomes non-existent.* No path is wrong, no person is wrong, no problem or judgment is wrong, nor is any of it right—it just is. *At a place of true enlightenment, you are simply in a place of being.* When you are one with God, everything is just as it should be…no matter what spiritual beliefs you have. It's all the same. We might even understand the worst "wrongdoing" as a violation of compassion for self and others….

When enlightenment is reached, we will understand that there really is no need to be healed because there is nothing to heal from or for. The mind can spin in circles. There is no wrong path and no problem that needs resolving because the power that created you will deliver all the solutions. But we cannot simply sit back and wait for God or this solution. A fine balance exists here where intentions still must be set; then they are placed in the lap of God to generate an effect. If we, in our limited self, imagined a solution, then perhaps that would be the extent of our awareness, but when we master the art of manifestation and experience the love of the creator for creation, infinite solutions are provided.

I want to share with you now one of my favorite stories about the balance between faith, logic, and reason:

I Sent You a Rowboat

> A very religious man was once caught in rising floodwaters. He climbed onto the roof of his house and trusted God to rescue him. A neighbor came by in a canoe and said, "The waters will soon be above your house. Hop in and we'll paddle to safety."
>
> "No thanks," replied the religious man. "I've prayed to God, so I'm sure He will save me."
>
> A short time later, the police came by in a boat. "The waters will soon be above your house. Hop in and we'll take you to safety."
>
> "No thanks," replied the religious man. "I've prayed to God, so I'm sure He will save me."

> A little time later, a rescue services helicopter hovered overhead, let down a rope ladder, and the pilot said, "The waters will soon be above your house. Climb the ladder and we'll fly you to safety."
>
> "No thanks," replied the religious man. "I've prayed to God, so I'm sure He will save me."
>
> All this time, the floodwaters continued to rise, until soon they reached above the roof and the religious man drowned. When he arrived in heaven, he demanded an audience with God. After being ushered into God's throne room, he said, "Lord, why am I here in heaven? I prayed for you to save me; I trusted you to save me from that flood."
>
> "Yes, you did, my child," replied the Lord. "And I sent you a canoe, a boat, and a helicopter. But you never got in."
>
> *Source: unknown*

Imagine yourself as a giant rolling wheel going through life…as the wheel rolls, sometimes it rolls through mud, gets wet, stops rolling, or gets banged or dented, but when it keeps rolling, it keeps having experiences. It can become part of a vehicle that is instrumental in transporting others or exist as a part of another whole. If the wheel stops, it's much harder to get it rolling again, and it can get stuck very deeply until someone pulls it out and sets it on its course again. A force greater than itself could possibly do much the same.

The way a true healer—or perhaps, we should refer to this person as an enlightened being—might work is simply working to set him or herself on a path to the divine; then others, witnessing that path, will follow. Various tools and methods are available to realign us, but ultimately, the experience should consist of methods of reconnecting us to the divine and becoming self-sourcing. Of course, all else may provide life lessons that end up directing us back on this path anyway. To give others true inspiration, we must first lead ourselves.

Over the years, many people have asked me whether they should take a particular yoga class or program, or they have asked me what to charge for yoga or healing services offered or classes taught. The answer is simple: You must have passion for what you do, and it must result in joy at every level of your existence, or why are you doing it to begin with? If there is joy, take or teach the class, but be realistic and cover your costs. Will there be a return on your investment? (It doesn't always have to be a financial return.) No matter what class you teach or take, the Law of Attraction is always in effect so each person there will be a reflection of your self. Notice: If you need to teach healing, then you may need a lot of healing yourself. If you need to take a class, then you are likely just not self-sourcing, or you are looking for new ways to learn how. You will always find the right teacher. The teacher is in the mirror…figuratively and literally. When this circular place of healing (healing what really doesn't need to be healed) and watching repeated patterns coming and going eventually becomes too chaotic, you can step outside of it all, watch it, and learn just to be. In a place of quiet, such as meditation, answers can be found, but ultimately, in the place of enlightenment, there really aren't any boundaries, rights, or wrongs—there is just a sense of being-ness. Have faith, listen to God, and just be.

Tips for Stepping Into Your Becoming:

1. Watch and heal from the patterns in your life.
2. Instead of resistance have compassion.
3. Love what is causing your resistance because it's there to teach you how to overcome something.
4. Melt into the problem or issue in your life and do not separate from it. It is all a part of the divine.
5. Believe you can heal.
6. Believe there is nothing wrong to begin with.

EXERCISE:

What patterns reappear in your life that cause you pain or discomfort? ____

____

____

____

____

____

Have you ever tried to love, or have compassion for, what you've spent so much time hating/dis-liking? Explain. ________________

____

____

____

____

____

Can you practice merging into what you'd like to heal and see the gifts in it? Can you find a way to see it as a part of the whole, the divine? ______________________________

Can you shift your beliefs into realizing that nothing is wrong with you? Can you see whatever you previously thought was wrong as part of your chosen life experiences to grow your soul? Explain. ________

AWAKEN — TRANSFORM — REALIZE

Chapter 16

Awakening

"Truth is that which time and space cannot prove wrong."

— Yogi Bhajan

Of course, to give in to the divine generally means going through some kind of life process that prepares you to free yourself from the confines of yourself. To free yourself from the programming of family beliefs, society, and your own developed habits takes time, strength, and trust in self and in something greater. It takes stepping deeply into your heart, releasing your ego, and having faith in self. When you trust in yourself and let the divine guide you, you become free to stand in your essence and in the freedom of your truth, and then you are forever awakened.

As Snatam Kaur says in a song she wrote for her daughter and anyone who takes the journey into his or her heart:

"You are becoming
The song of your heart
How beautiful it is
As the flower blossoms forth
Feel the earth in your toes
Oh my child you'll never know
What tomorrow brings
So sing, sing, sing
Rise before the morning light
Let your soul take its flight
God is with you listening
So sing, sing, sing
Hand in hand we shall go
Through the grassy hills of gold
See the hawk circling
We sing, sing, sing
You are becoming
The song of your heart
How beautiful it is
As the flower blossoms forth."

Awakening Others

To find the true awakened state of self is to know that nothing can rattle you into believing you are anything less than a mirror of the divine. As perceived problems and issues come into your life, you know you are guided by the power that created you; you also know that all those you may worry about are also being guided and led at each stage…and their timing may not match the pace of yours, but it all is happening in the appropriate time for each person.

You cannot truly "fix" someone else, but you can lead by powerful and connected examples. Each being must step into his or her awakened state at his or her own pace. We all have individual life paths and a personal journey to make, and it's all based on divine timing. Each person steps through his or her life journey as planned before incarnation. There is no need to have guilt, worry, or perceived failure if someone is not awakening as you have, as quickly as you have, or using the same technologies you have. A flower only blooms when the conditions are optimal.

One of the most frustrating parts of my life for many years was that I wished others would be on the same journey I was. I wished others I loved were awakened. I grew angry when they judged me for awakening in the ways I had. I grew angry when I couldn't talk to them about the things that awakened and thrilled me to no end. I was sad that my interests weren't shared. I even lost interest in my interests when others didn't express the same love for my loves. During these times, I didn't hold true to myself and felt hopeless because I was becoming aware of things that many on our planet didn't find equally amazing. I dimmed the light of many of my psychic gifts to fit in because what I was seeing and experiencing wasn't the "norm," and I also didn't understand the point of having these gifts. I didn't know how they served me or others. I felt I was opening to things that would scare people if I shared them. The knowledge I was gaining was not easy to share without judgment, ridicule, and huge uphill battles. Of course, now I know that was also part of my life plan.

But the truth is that these experiences were intended for me and not for other people in my social circles. I understood it was best to have the experience and move on, knowing it was a special experience meant simply for me. It really makes you start to see the little gifts God sends just for you when you look at things this way. Some loneliness can exist in the place of spirit when you divide your spiritual experiences from others, but no separation really exists because God is within all. I've learned I don't have to go into a spiritual community to have a spiritual experience, just as I don't have to step into personal meditation to connect to something greater. I can simply allow the God spirit to flow through me in all things at all times. There is no separation. God is in all.

I see the world awakening in small ways. And I see the majority still move with the masses, unknowingly dulling their fullest potential by not asking questions, not challenging systems that don't work, not speaking up, not telling their truths, and not sharing their stories. I admit I still feel frustrated that as a whole our world remains unaware of the healing powers in nature, the concept of having compassion verses competition, and the labeling of yoga and energy healing as "alternative" forms of care. I stepped away from my roles as yoga teacher and healer partly because of this frustration, but I also stepped away to heal, more deeply discover my truths, and understand what would best serve me moving forward. I needed to serve myself before I could serve others.

I was also seeking balance, and I was trying to find a way in which all my practices could exist in my every day and not just in a role I played. I struggled trying to understand what to do with my psychic awareness and my spiritual practices. I found them very separate from the rest of the world for many years. For me, it took time to find the balance. But I never had the "look" of a healer nor of an executive. I didn't care to blend into either environment. I hadn't fit in in my entire life. At this point, I know I don't care to because in my truth I could never fit in and never will want to. We are all meant to be unique essences of Self. We are meant to find our gifts and share them with the world…no matter what they are!

I believe we are all meant to be healers of self. Once we master that, we can assist others in finding their own paths. Ultimately, we need to find what brings us joy from that connected place within and share our gifts with the world with a goal of making it a better place to live.

"Love pours forth from the hearth of the Universe."

— Snatam Kaur

If you are a light worker (or a conscious being) and heal people with energy, then you attract certain people to you like a magnet. If someone asks you for help through healing, she is asking you to help yourself break down a barrier that she also has. She has been attracted to you simply to show you the mirror of yourself. When you find that mirror within yourself, you develop compassion for self and compassion for the other. You are grateful for having been shown where enhancements can be made in your life. If you are aware of this concept, you don't have to call yourself a light worker or a healer. In that place of conscious awareness, you are ultimately awakening others. It can be a subtle or truly divine experience. As we go through life as conscious mindful beings, we seize the opportunities to heal ourselves because we ultimately know that doing so heals the rest of the planet. Understand that the concepts of quantum physics mean we are all one, and in that place of oneness, one person can break out of the cocoon and start the butterfly effect to heal our planet. So, yes, one person can truly make a difference!

Awakening Universally

We'd be foolish to believe we are all alone on our planet, left without help from the power that created us, but we'd be equally as foolish to believe we were all alone in the universe. Quantum physics basically proves we are all one here on earth, but what if we were to take that idea further? What if we had a brotherhood or sisterhood watching over us like angels of heaven? What if we weren't alone and our thoughts, beliefs, and visions were broadcast into that collective consciousness soup? And what if someone learned how to read those aspects of self to learn more about us? And what if our brothers and sisters were not that far away and wanted to interact with us? What if all our essence (our thoughts, patterns, likes and dislikes, habits, and wounds) went into a kind of matrix that floated over us like a network of phone lines wrapping around the planet? And what if this matrix were infinite and not limited to time, date, or place? What if in this place all logic and history resided?

Perhaps our souls' experiences exist in textbooks (the Akashic records, per se?), and we can learn from repeated patterns of our lives past? Perhaps stepping into our becoming means cleaning up our personal vibrations and preparing ourselves for contact with other worlds or other beings? Perhaps we are kept in the dark here on planet Earth, and the rest of the solar system and beyond is watching how we go about finding the light switch in the dark? Perhaps our life is just a test? Are you able to find the light switch to your soul? And when you find that switch, are you prepared for what you will see? Have you done your work? Have you honestly lived your life the best way you can? If you met another being from another place in another galaxy, would you be able to communicate truly about life, our planet, and our species as a whole, or would you only know how to tell them about how to buy something on the Internet, how hard you work, who your favorite purse designer is, or what kind of car you drive? Would you truly understand how to share the essence of self, man, and our planet?

Tips for Stepping Into Your Becoming:

1. Release your ego.
2. Have faith in self.
3. Be the master of your own truth.
4. Believe: God is within all. God is within all. God is within all!
5. Know we are all one.

EXERCISE:

Practice living by seeing others as glowing balls of light rather than as physical beings with hair and clothing. Watch as all preconceived beliefs fall away and you let go of ego and judgment, and replace them with compassion. Describe your experience. ____________________

____
____
____
____
____
____
____
____
____

AWAKEN — TRANSFORM — REALIZE

A Final Note:

Being in Your Awakened State

"When one realizes one is asleep,
at that moment one is already half-awake."

— Pyotr Uspensky

If you had just one life (this one), you were in a perfectly healed state, your limits were removed, and you were opened to infinite possibilities, could you say you were living the best life you could dream into being for yourself? For others? If not, what would you let go of? What would you change? What steps would you take to remove perceived obstacles and live your life in abundance? What does prosperity look like to you?

In this book, we have walked through awakening, into transformation, realizing, and finally, being. I shared some of my stories of stepping into my becoming. I shared how change, loss, love, and anger can motivate you to make a change in your life. I shared how life challenges can cause you to have more faith, and how by stepping deeper into that faith, you can step into your healed self. I shared how once you begin to see your healed self as never wounded, you begin to walk deeper into the understanding that love is the ultimate truth. When you open to love, you begin to realize you are not alone and the power that created you is there to support you. You begin to see that answers can be found in nature, and that nature is here to comfort, love, and guide you on your path. When you realize all this, you see deeper into the consciousness of self and the collective, and you begin to understand deeper levels of love and happiness and how to be you authentically. Not only will your belief in yourself then be stronger, but you'll more deeply understand the power behind that belief and of living in the now; that understanding will then help you develop your own principles to live by. Through the process, you will learn to have patience on your journey and heal yourself.

My goal with this book has been to open your awareness to the fact that by no fault of your own, you have been living your life under self-imposed limitations and perceived blockages. My goal was to teach you that you have all the power to step out of "the system"—out of depression, out of old ways, out of pain, and out of what isn't working—by simply making the choice to do so. Just make the choice! Wake up to the possibilities of the divine power within you, and know that the power you came from supports and loves you! Our world is ready for a change, so let that change start with you!

"If we could change ourselves,
the tendencies in the world would also change.
As a man changes his own nature,
so does the attitude of the world change towards him.
We need not wait to see what others do."

— Mahatma Gandhi

I have learned a lot as I have written this book, and I hope you have learned as you read it. I wrote this book with great love in hopes of healing my broken heart from the wounds of my past. I gained a new awareness as the words hit the pages and gave me a new appreciation of self and a richer, deeper love for others and the planet. So now the challenge is yours. I challenge you to get out a piece of paper and answer the following questions.

- What if you make a list of your wounds, un-identify with them and let them go?
- What if you upgrade your faith to match your destiny?
- What if you let go of your ego, pride, and material things, and listen to your heart?
- What if you let go of social conditioning and start looking for your own answers?
- What if you stop following the crowd and live in your own essence?
- What if you choose knowledge over veils of ignorance?
- What if you truly have compassion for yourself? For others?
- What if you are thankful for losses in your life?
- What if you allowed traumas to turn into miracles?
- What if you overcame doubt and believed in miracles?
- What if you listen to the earth speak to you?
- What if you took the time to learn new healing methods or philosophies?
- What if you saw yourself in the reflection of others?
- What if you walked your story through a healing method instead

of playing into the drama?

- What if you stepped out of the depression and into yourself?
- What if nature could help you find your essence?
- What if you could truly dream your world into being?
- What if you were honest about your thoughts?
- What if you stopped watching television and started a conscious practice to find and strengthen your self?
- What if you listened to something spoken from divine masters and brought it into a facet of your life instead of just reading it?
- What if you could master your desires?
- What if you could end your suffering?
- What if your beliefs could be the power to change your life?
- What if you just had a little faith?
- What if you decided to unlearn false beliefs and utilize your true power?
- What if you stopped asking for something in prayer and prayed from your soul?
- What if you no longer had to wrestle with doubt?
- What if you no longer believed in lack and stepped into abundance?
- What if all the answers to life could be self-sourced?
- What if you could find your power in a place of powerlessness?
- What if you lived in the now?
- What if you had patience and allowed for divine timing?

- What if every student became a teacher?
- What if every leader taught with divine principles?
- What if God wasn't coming to save you but you had to save yourself?
- What if you became a conscious and compassionate person and stepped into your own becoming?
- What if you forgave yourself and others you once blamed or judged?
- What if you meditated?
- What if you stopped complaining about our leaders and became one yourself?

I don't expect you to resonate with everything in this book, but I do hope I have helped you conquer yourself with just one word or paragraph you've read here. My goal is not necessarily to shift you into some new religion or practice, but I do hope I have helped you think differently about how you choose to live your life. Your choices and beliefs matter more than you might have realized. You do make a difference. You are important, and your opinions matter.

I want you to write to tell me where you are in your life and how you need help or support. I can get you started in the right direction as you step into your becoming. I'm also available to discuss death, loss, and your grieving process. I can help point you in the direction of a Kundalini yoga teacher or Shamanic healer in your area. I am available to teach Kundalini yoga, Shamanic healing, and vegan diet and nutrition. If you are interested in bringing me in to work with you personally, or to speak or teach at a retreat in your area, I would like to help you in your transformation. If you'd like to write your own book, I would love to help you share your story as well. Please contact me via text at (808) 280.5559 and/or connect with me on social media.

I challenge you to step passionately into your becoming, have faith, trust in God, believe in yourself, and have compassion for others. I wish you a big, warm Maui aloha, love, hugs, success, and support on your path to stepping into your becoming and finding that beautiful person you came here to be! I will hold you in my heart and create a sacred space of goodwill for you to step into your becoming.

Blessings On Your Journey! A hui ho! (Hawaiian for "Until we meet again.")

I will finish by giving you this typical blessing in Hawaiian: *E pili mau na pomaika'i me 'oe*; "May you always have good fortune," or simply, "Best wishes."

Much Love,

Nicole Gabriel

AWAKEN — TRANSFORM — REALIZE

ABOUT THE AUTHOR

NICOLE GABRIEL, MBA, is an author, professional speaker, graphic designer, life coach, and animal grief counselor. She is also a vegan nutrition coach. She has been a student and teacher of Peruvian Shamanism and Kundalini yoga (RYT500) for many years. She is a raw vegan food enthusiast, seeker of truth, animal rights advocate, supporter of women in technology, and owner of Vegan Dog Treats and Angel Dog Productions. As a former auto executive from Detroit, she holds an MBA in Technology Management. She is Certified in Transpersonal Psychology at the Master's Level, has a B.A. in Communications, and a degree in Graphic Design and Commercial Art.

For more than twenty years, she has studied business, personal growth and development, spirituality, health, nutrition, and wellness. She spent nearly a decade traveling the world in search of herself after a series of life-changing events—spending time in Central and South America working with shamanic healers, and more locally, studying the yogic philosophies of, in particular, Kundalini yoga.

Prior to retiring from a six-figure income in corporate America at age thirty-two, Nicole spent a decade in web-related technology management, marketing, and advertising as a "Big 3" automotive executive in Detroit. She followed that experience by successfully building and growing a $1.2 million per year chiropractic/spa franchise in three locations throughout Michigan.

Today, she lives on Maui, Hawaii, with her fiancé, Patrick, their English Bulldog and Chinese Shar Peis. Among other things, she runs her businesses, Vegan Dog Treats (a healthy dog snack alternative) and Angel Dog Productions (designing websites, book covers, speaker presentations, and logos for aspiring new business owners and authors).

Let Nicole Help Guide
You into Stepping into Your Becoming!

www.NicoleKristinGabriel.com

(808) 280-5559

ABOUT PET GRIEF COUNSELLING

Have you lost your best friend? Does it feel like no one can understand the pain of your loss? You and I know that we haven't just lost our pet! Our "hairy children" are not only our best friends, but they are accepted into our lives sometimes as substitutes for a partner, child, or other companion. They are solidly there during traumatic or emotional times in our lives. They are our loyal companions and sometimes the only ones there for us when everyone else walks away. And their loss can really break our hearts!

Whether you have lost a dog, cat, rabbit, or horse, Nicole would like to offer you a no-obligation, complimentary 30-60 minute consultation to help you heal from your grief. Please contact her (call or text). With her help, you will get through this grieving process and heal your pain.

Nicole has lost many of her companions, and after coping with the initial grief of the loss, she eventually found the strength she wants to share with you...to help you heal. Let her be someone to talk to during this time of great mourning and change.

www.NicoleKristinGabriel.com
(808) 280-5559

AWAKEN — TRANSFORM — REALIZE

ABOUT ANGEL DOG PRODUCTIONS

Nicole Gabriel has spent twenty-plus years in the arts, doing advertising, marketing, and website development, among other things. She began her other business (Vegan Dog Treats) with the help of her canine companion Shiitake. The brand needed a label, so Nicole started there. The logo was born with a cartoon image of Shiitake on the bag, website, and business cards. After a short period, people started asking who did the creative work. Soon, Angel Dog Productions was born.

Angel Dog Productions (ADP) designs book covers, interior book layout, websites, logos, and images that are used for personal or corporate branding. Much of the focus for Nicole's clients is to get them set up with a "look" to launch their book, speaking, and marketing campaigns. Nicole also creates speaker presentations. ADP's goal in creating websites is to make the content simple and easy to manage for the owner. Nicole loves what she does and loves helping people, so please look her up. She'd love to hear from you! Call or text for a no-obligation, complimentary 30-60 minute consultation.

www.AngelDogProductions.com

AWAKEN — TRANSFORM — REALIZE

ABOUT VEGAN DOG TREATS

After nearly a decade of watching her dogs struggle with daily and terminal health issues, Nicole Gabriel successfully created a new way to feed pets that is not only good for them, but a humane approach that leaves a smaller global footprint on the planet and doesn't require the taking of a life.

Dogs are classified as omnivores and are scavengers by nature. All the ingredients in Vegan Dog Treats are organic, natural, all vegan, and raw. The ingredients are kept primarily intact when they are not heated, which means they keep their nutrients. Flavors include: (Visit the website for the latest flavors.)

Peanut Butter & Jelly: Made with Maui Kula Strawberries and fresh organic peanut butter.

Coconut Banana: Great for bones, joints, skin, and hair.

Pumpkin: High in antioxidants.

Cheezy Veggie: Made with nutritional yeast and bell peppers, and also high in antioxidants.

If you're going to feed your dog a snack, why not make it a healthy alternative that doesn't require killing one to serve another? It just makes sense!

www.Vegan-DogTreats.com
www.NicoleKristinGabriel.com
(808) 280-5559

ABOUT SHAMANIC HEALING & YOGA TEACHING

During her travels to Peru, Bolivia, and other locations in Central and South America, while working with shamanic healers, Nicole was told she would be a great healer and teacher, and through her life experiences, she would excel. In her yoga, she would be told that to master something was to teach it. So you could say she's still seeking mastery.

If you have always wanted to know how to heal yourself or another through shamanic healing techniques, Nicole teaches a series of classes that will start you on your way.

She is also available (as Nirankar Kaur) to teach Kundalini yoga. She is available as a guest teacher, lecturer, meditation guide, or "humanology philosopher" for your organization, studio, or center. Call or text for a no-obligation, complimentary 30-60 minute consultation.

www.NicoleKristinGabriel.com
(808) 280-5559

AWAKEN — TRANSFORM — REALIZE

ABOUT LIFE, NUTRITION, AND WELLNESS COACHING

Are you unhappy at work? Are you always tired and lacking energy? Have you put on a few pounds and your jeans no longer fit? Are you suffering from emotional or physical pain? Are you stressed and looking for both career and relationship solutions? Personal growth and development has been a keen subject of interest for Nicole Gabriel her whole life. While others her age were out doing silly teenager things, she was sitting at home reading books from self-help authors. From there, her interests flowed into diet and then spirituality.

Let Nicole show you how to move from tragedy, loss, death, or change into a better you! With certification in Transpersonal Psychology and several years of alternative therapy practice and research, Nicole will listen and help you through whatever stage of life you are experiencing. She can discuss diet for you and/or your pet. The light is just around the corner, so let's just find the switch! Your wellness is within reach. Call or text for a no-obligation, complimentary 30-60 minute consultation.

www.NicoleKristinGabriel.com
(808) 280-5559

AWAKEN — TRANSFORM — REALIZE

BOOK NICOLE GABRIEL TO SPEAK AT YOUR NEXT EVENT

When it comes to choosing a compassionate speaker for your next event, you'll find no one more capable of transforming your audience than Nicole. She will take your hand and lead you on a transformational journey. Her stories are inspiring, comical, tragic, and mysterious—yet, at the same time, by having just a little faith, you will be transported into a magical sacred space where the big "ahas" happen.

Whether your audience is 10 or 10,000, in North America or abroad, Nicole Gabriel will deliver a tailor-made message of inspiration for your meeting, conference, or classroom. Speaking topics include:

- Embracing Change
- Becoming a Leader from Within
- Transforming Your Life
- Letting Go and Having Faith
- Peruvian Shamanism Theories & Practice
- Kundalini Yoga Theories & Practice

- Becoming Vegan
- Eating Food as Medicine
- Learning from Animals
- Defining Self

www.NicoleKristinGabriel.com
(808) 280-5559